T0220713

Make Your Own Python Text Adventure

A Guide to Learning Programming

Phillip Johnson

Apress®

Make Your Own Python Text Adventure

Phillip Johnson
New York, USA

ISBN-13 (pbk): 978-1-4842-3230-9
https://doi.org/10.1007/978-1-4842-3231-6

ISBN-13 (electronic): 978-1-4842-3231-6

Library of Congress Control Number: 2017960887

Cover image designed by Freepik

Managing Director: Welmoed Spahr
Editorial Director: Todd Green
Acquisitions Editor: Todd Green
Development Editor: James Markham
Technical Reviewer: Tri Phan
Coordinating Editor: Jill Balzano
Copy Editor: Kezia Endsley
Compositor: SPi Global
Indexer: SPi Global
Artist: SPi Global

Distributed to the book trade worldwide by Springer Science+Business Media New York, 233 Spring Street, 6th Floor, New York, NY 10013. Phone 1-800-SPRINGER, fax (201) 348-4505, e-mail orders-ny@springer-sbm.com, or visit www.springeronline.com. Apress Media, LLC is a California LLC and the sole member (owner) is Springer Science + Business Media Finance Inc (SSBM Finance Inc). SSBM Finance Inc is a **Delaware** corporation.

For information on translations, please e-mail rights@apress.com, or visit http://www.apress.com/rights-permissions.

Apress titles may be purchased in bulk for academic, corporate, or promotional use. eBook versions and licenses are also available for most titles. For more information, reference our Print and eBook Bulk Sales web page at http://www.apress.com/bulk-sales.

Any source code or other supplementary material referenced by the author in this book is available to readers on GitHub via the book's product page, located at www.apress.com/9781484232309. For more detailed information, please visit http://www.apress.com/source-code.

Printed on acid-free paper

Table of Contents

About the Author

Phillip Johnson is a software developer based out of Columbus, Ohio. He has worked on projects ranging from call center queuing to bioinformatics and has used a wide range of technologies, including Python, Java, Scala, and SQL. He blogs at Let's Talk Data (http://letstalkdata.com).

About the Technical Reviewer

Tri Phan is the founder of the Programming Learning Channel on YouTube. He has over 10 years of experience in the software industry. He has outsourced for many companies and can write applications in many fields and in many programming languages, including PHP, Java, and C #. In addition, he has over 10 years of experience teaching at international programming training centers like Aptech, NIIT, and Kent College.

About the Technical Reviewer

CHAPTER 1

Getting Started

Introduction

So you've heard the Internet chanting, "Learn to code! Learn to code!", and you've read that Python is a good place to start...but now what? Many people who want to program don't know where to start. The idea that you can create "anything" with code is paralyzing. This book provides a clear goal: learn Python by creating a text adventure.

This book will teach you the fundamentals of programming, including how to organize code and some coding best practices. By the end of the book, you will have a working game that you can play or show off to friends. You will also be able to change the game and make it your own by writing a different story line, including adding new items, creating new characters, etc.

Learning to program is an exciting endeavor, but can feel daunting at first. However, if you stick with it, you could become a professional programmer or a weekend hobbyist, or both! My story is similar to the stories of many programmers: The first thing I programmed was a number guessing game in QBASIC and now programming is my job. I hope that you, too, can join us, and I thank you for choosing this book as the place to start.

© Phillip Johnson 2018
P. Johnson, *Make Your Own Python Text Adventure*,
https://doi.org/10.1007/978-1-4842-3231-6_1

Who This Book Is For

This book is intended for people who have never programmed before or for novice programmers starting out with Python. If you're in this second group, you can probably skim some of the early material.

Although this is geared toward beginners, I do make some assumptions that you know computer basics such as opening a command prompt, installing software, etc. If you get stuck on anything, an Internet search for "how to do [thing] on [operating system]" will typically help you out. Particularly useful web sites for programmers are StackOverflow (`http://stackoverflow.com`)[1] and SuperUser (`http://superuser.com`),[2] so if you see them in your search results, give them a shot first.

How To Use This Book

In each chapter of the book, you will make progress on the overall goal of creating your text adventure. The early chapters may seem like slow going because they focus on learning the basics of Python. Things will pick up in the second half of the book, when the focus shifts toward building the game world.

I suggest reading this book on or beside your computer so you can easily go back and forth between reading and writing code. Each of the chapters in the first half of the book will end with a homework section. These problems won't be required for the main game, but you should at least try them. When applicable, solutions are provided at the end of the book.

Most of the Python code in this book will look like this:

```
1   greeting = "Hello, World!"
2   print(greeting)
```

---

[1] `http://stackoverflow.com`
[2] `http://superuser.com`

Code that is intended to be entered into an interactive Python session (see Chapter 3) will look like this:

```
>>> greeting = "Hello, World!"
>>> print(greeting)
```

References to code or commands that appear inline will appear like this. Technical terms that you should learn *appear like this*.

If you ever get stuck, you can download the code for each chapter in the book here.[3] Resist the urge to copy and paste everything! You'll retain more information if you type out the code. However, we all make mistakes, so if you can't figure out what's wrong, you can compare your code against mine. If you're really sure everything is the same, double-check with an online comparison tool like DiffChecker[4] or Mergely.[5] You can also check Appendix B for some common errors you may run into.

Finally, this game is your game. It is fully customizable, and if you feel comfortable adding more rooms and enemies, changing the story, making it more difficult, etc., please do so. I will point out good customization opportunities like this:

 Customization Point   Some notes about customization.

Keep in mind that each chapter builds on the last, so if you deviate too far from the material, you may want to save your customized code in another directory so you can keep learning from the source material.

---

[3]https://www.dropbox.com/sh/udvdkxtjhtlqdh1/AAD9HOD6VTb5RGFZ7k Bv-ghua?dl=0
[4]https://www.diffchecker.com
[5]http://www.mergely.com/editor

Setting Up Your Workspace

Don't skip this section! You need to make sure everything is set up properly before you begin working on the code in this book. A lot of problems await you if you have an improper configuration.

Python Versions

The creators of Python made a decision that Python 3 would not be backwards compatible with Python 2. And while Python 3 was released in 2008, some people still cling to Python 2. There's no reason for beginners to start out with Python 2, so this book is written using Python 3. Unfortunately, some operating systems are bundled with Python 2, which can make installing and using Python 3 a bit tricky. If you run into trouble, there are plenty of detailed instructions for your specific operating system online.

Installing Python

There are many ways to install Python depending on your operating system and what (if any) package managers you use.

Windows

An advantage of installing Python on Windows is that you don't need to worry about an already existing old version. Windows does not have a standard package manager, so you'll need to download the installer from Python.

1. Open `http://python.org/download/` in your browser and download the latest 3.x.y installer for Windows.

2. Run the installer.

3. On the first screen of the installer, you will see an option to include Python 3.X on the PATH. Be sure to check that box.

4. Proceed through the installation; the default settings are fine. If you see another option in the installer for Add Python to Environment Variables, make sure that box is checked too.

Mac OS X

From my experience, the easiest way to install developer tools on Mac OS X is by using the Homebrew[6] package manager (http://brew.sh). However, I appreciate that you may not want to install something to install something else! I'll provide the Homebrew steps first and then the more traditional path.

Using Homebrew:

1. Open a terminal.

2. Install Homebrew by running the command at http://brew.sh in the terminal.

3. Install Python 3 with the following command: brew install python3.

You will now use the command python3 anytime you want to use Python. The command python points to the default Mac OS X installation of Python, which is version 2.7.5.

---

[6]http://brew.sh

Using the Installer:

1. Open `http://python.org/download/` in your
    browser and download the latest 3.x.y installer for
    Mac OS X.

2. Open the download package and then run
    `Python.mpkg`.

3. Follow the installation wizard. The default settings
    are fine.

You will now use the command `python3` anytime you want to use
Python. The command `python` points to the default Mac OS X installation
of Python, which is version 2.7.5.

Linux

If you're using Linux, chances are you are already comfortable using your
distribution's package manager, so I won't go into details. Typically, something
like `sudo apt-get install python3` or `sudo yum install python3` will
get what you want. It is also possible that your distribution already includes
Python 3. If all else fails, you can download the source and build Python from
the official web site (`https://www.python.org/downloads/source/`).[7]

Verify Your Installation

To verify your installation, open a command prompt/terminal (I'll use
console, command prompt, and terminal interchangeably) and try both of
these commands:

```
python --version
python3 --version
```

---

[7]`https://www.python.org/downloads/source/`

There are four possibilities:

- *Both display a version number:* Great, you have both Python 2 and 3 installed on your computer. Just make sure you always run the code in this book with python3.

- *Only Python displays a version number:* If the first number in the version is a 3, as in "Python 3.5.1" you are OK. If instead it is a Python 2 version, as in "Python 2.7.10", then Python 3 is not properly installed. Try repeating the installation and if that still does not work, you may need to adjust your PATH to point to Python 3 instead of Python 2.

- *Only Python3 displays a version number:* Great, you have Python 3 installed. Just make sure you always run the code in this book with python3.

- *Neither displays a version number:* Python is not properly installed. Try repeating the installation. If that still does not work, you may need to adjust your PATH to include the location of your Python installation.

CHAPTER 2

Your First Program

When you open an application on your computer, such as an Internet browser, at the lowest level the CPU is executing instructions to move around bytes of information. Early programs were painstakingly written on punch cards, as shown in Figure 2-1.

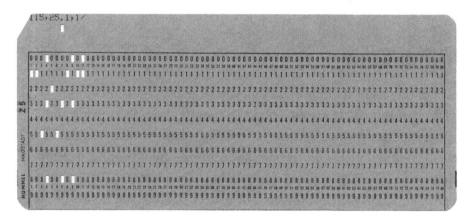

Figure 2-1. *An early punch card Credit: Wikipedia user Harke*

Thankfully, we have decades of improvements to computer programming that make it much easier to write those instructions! Now, programming languages lie on a spectrum of "lower-level" to "higher-level" with languages like C and C++ being lower-level and languages like Python and Ruby being higher-level. By design, higher-level languages allow programmers to ignore much of the behind-the-scenes details of computer programs. This is one reason why Python is often recommended as a first programming language.

© Phillip Johnson 2018
P. Johnson, *Make Your Own Python Text Adventure*,
https://doi.org/10.1007/978-1-4842-3231-6_2

To get started, create a folder on your computer where you will do all of the work for your game. From here on out, this directory will be referred to as the *root* directory of your project.

Creating a Module

Python code is organized into files called *modules*. Each module usually contains a significant amount of code that is all logically related. For example, our project will contain a module that runs the game, another module that contains the code for managing the enemies, another for the world, etc. To create your first module, navigate to your root directory and create an empty file called game.py.

Writing Code

When writing code, it's important that you write the code *exactly* as it appears in this book. However, I don't recommend simply copying and pasting. Especially when starting out, muscle memory will help you learn faster. If you run into errors, review your code line-by-line and check for typos, wrong casing, misplaced symbols, etc. If you really can't figure out the problem, then and only then is it okay to copy code. But always be sure to read over the pasted code to find your error.

I need to mention here one of the more controversial parts of the Python syntax: meaningful whitespace. Many languages ignore spaces and tabs, but Python does not. This means that you can run into problems caused by characters you can't (easily) see! Because of that, you need to decide if you will use tabs or spaces to indent your code. Most Python programmers have chosen to use spaces, so I will stick with the convention of using four spaces to indent the code for this book. *If you choose to use tabs and copy code you must switch the indentation to tabs!* Some text editors can do this for you with a toolbar command. If yours does not, you should be able to replace four spaces with "\t" (which means "tab").

With that in mind, let's write your first line of code. Open game.py and add the following line:

```
print("Escape from Cave Terror!")
```

 Customization Point

You can change the name of your game by replacing the text inside the quotation marks. Think about the scene your game takes place in. Is it a medieval forest, an alien spaceship, or a crime-ridden city?

Running Python Programs

Now, we'll execute the code we just wrote. Start by opening a command prompt or terminal and then use the cd command to navigate to your project root directory. For example, cd ~/Documents/code/learn-python-game or cd C:\Code\my_python_adventure. Finally, run the following command:

```
python game.py
```

(**Note**: Depending on how you installed Python, you may need to run python3 game.py.)

If all went well, you should see "Escape from Cave Terror!" printed out to the console. Congratulations! You just wrote your first Python program.

Homework

Try the following exercise for homework:

1. Make a new module called `calculator.py` and write code that will print out "`Which numbers do you want to add?`" to the console.

2. Run the calculator program and make sure it works correctly.

3. Try removing the quotes from the code. What happens?

CHAPTER 3

Listening to Your Users

All computer programs have some level of user input. Some may simply require a user to start the application, while others simply wait patiently until a user tells it to do something. Since this application is a text adventure, it falls closer to the "wait patiently" end of the spectrum. In this chapter, you'll learn how to read and process instructions that the user types into the command prompt.

Your Friends: stdout and stdin

By definition, text adventures require the user to enter text instructions for the program. In response, the program will display text to the user. This is a common pattern in command-line applications.

To get a feel for this, let's demo a command-line application that you already have installed—Python. That's right, the python command can do more than just run programs. Open your command prompt and run python. You should see something like this:

```
$ python
Python 3.4.1 (default, May 8 2015, 22:07:39)
[GCC 4.2.1 Compatible Apple LLVM 6.1.0 (clang-602.0.49)] on
darwin
```

© Phillip Johnson 2018
P. Johnson, *Make Your Own Python Text Adventure*,
https://doi.org/10.1007/978-1-4842-3231-6_3

```
Type "help", "copyright", "credits" or "license" for more
information.
>>>
```

Now, at the cursor, type this and press Enter:

```
help(print)
```

You should see this:

```
>>> help(print)

Help on built-in function print in module builtins:

[...]
```

To exit this view, simply press q.

We just interacted with this command-line application by entering two commands: help(print) and q. Both of those commands were read in by Python, interpreted, and responded to.

When an application writes out text to the console, this is called writing to *standard output* or *stdout* for short. Similarly, when a user (or even another application) writes text into the console, it is called writing to *standard input* or *stdin*.

In fact, if you go back to the console and type help(print) again, you'll see that the documentation refers to sys.stdout. By default, the print function writes text to standard output. You already saw this in action when you ran the game—the application displayed the intro text to the console.

Now try entering help(input). You can read that the input function will "read a string from *standard input*." This is exactly what we're looking for to allow our application to listen to the user.

To exit, press q and then type quit(). This should take you back to a regular command prompt.

Reading from Standard Input

Open a new file and save it as echo.py. Enter the following line:

```
input("Type some text: ")
```

Save the file and run it using python echo.py. Remember, to run an application, you must be at the same directory in which the file is contained.

Hopefully, you see the prompt "Type some text". Go ahead and do as it says, then press Enter. It might seem like the program ignored you and tossed you back to the command prompt. So what just happened? The input command printed out the prompt text ("Type some text") to standard output, and it read in your response to standard input. Since there were no more instructions, the application simply exited.

As the name of the file hinted, we're going to make an application that echoes back to the user, but first we need to learn how to store temporary information.

Saving Information

In the last exercise, we were able to read in information from the user, but we weren't able to do anything with it. We need to save that input temporarily so we can print it out. Temporary information can be stored in and accessed from a computer's memory using *variables*.

Some examples of variable names in Python are n, my_number, and address. To store information in a variable, we simply use the = operator. This is called the *assignment operator*. For example:

```
1   n = 5
2   my_number = 3
3   address = '123 Maple St.'
```

Then, anytime we need to recall that information, we can refer to the variable name as in print(n) or print(address). Let's get some practice.

Return to your terminal and run python. When we did this before, we used the help command to get information about functions. Perhaps a more useful feature is the ability to enter Python code and have it executed immediately. This is called the "Python interpreter", "Python shell" or "Python REPL" (abbreviation of *Read Evaluate Print Loop*).

Go ahead and enter the following commands:

```
>>> address = '123 Maple St.'
>>> print(address)
```

You should see "123 Maple St." printed out. This works because we *assigned* the value "123 Maple St." using the *assignment* operator to the variable address. Then when the print function runs, it looks up the real value of address in memory so it knows what to print out.

With this information, we can now do something more interesting with our echo program. Go back to echo.py and change the code as follows:

```
1   user_input = input("Type some text: ")
2   print(user_input)
```

Run this program again and verify that it echoes back whatever text you enter. Let's do something similar to our game. Open game.py and add the following lines:

```
2   action_input = input('Action: ')
3   print(action_input)
```

Data Types

Before we finish this chapter, we need to briefly go over some data types. So far, we've mostly seen textual data like "Type some text" and "123 Maple St.". These are called *strings*[1] and Python knows they are strings because they are surrounded by single or double quotes in the code. The data that input returns is also a string. Here are some examples of strings:

```
1   name = 'Phillip'
2   forecast = "It's going to rain!"
3   url = 'http://letstalkdata.com'
```

The next most common data type is the *integer*. If you remember from math class, integers are numbers like 1, 15, -99, and 0. In Python, integers are entered as numbers without any extra symbols.

```
1   a = 3
2   b = 4
3   hypotenuse = 5
```

A number that has a decimal point is called a *floating point* number or a *float* for short. Floats are entered similarly to integers, except they contain decimal points.

```
1   a = 3.0
2   b = 4.0
3   hypotenuse = 5.0
```

---

[1]Internally, Python stores text data in a variety of different formats. The most common you will encounter are str and bytes. Thus the word "string" does not always correlate exactly with the Python str type.

You can perform basic math operations on numbers just like you would expect. Try out some of these in the interpreter:

```
>>> 5 + 6
>>> 0 - 99
>>> 5.0 / 2.0
>>> 5 / 2
>>> 4 * (7 - 2)
```

There are many, many more data types that Python has built-in, but for now the important thing to notice is that Python infers the types based on how you type them. There's a big difference between my_variable = 5 and my_variable = '5'!

Homework

Try the following exercises for homework:

1. What *is* the difference between my_variable = 5 and my_variable = '5'?

2. What is the difference between print(n) and print('n')? If you're not sure, try entering the following commands into the Python interpreter:

    ```
    n = 5
    print(n)
    print('n')
    ```

3. Try rewriting echo.py without using a variable.

CHAPTER 4

Decisions

You have a big decision to make tomorrow—take the bus or walk. Okay, well, maybe not so much a *big* decision, but a decision nonetheless. Your decision could be made based on a number of factors, but let's keep it simple. If it rains, then you will take the bus; otherwise, you will walk.

Notice the structure of the decision:

1. First, there is something that is either true or false. In this case, the thing that is true or false is the presence or absence of rain. This is called a *condition*.

2. Next, there is an action taken if the condition is true. If it is raining, then you take the bus.

3. Finally, there is an action taken if the condition is false. If it is not raining, then you walk.

Computers need the ability make decisions in the same way. In computer code, we can give the computer a condition to evaluate and actions to take if that condition is true or false. This concept is called *branching* because code can "branch" into two or more directions when we need it to.

© Phillip Johnson 2018
P. Johnson, *Make Your Own Python Text Adventure*,
https://doi.org/10.1007/978-1-4842-3231-6_4

Booleans

Formally, a statement that is either true or false is called a *boolean expression*. Here are some examples of boolean expressions:

- My age in years is 30

- I have two siblings

- 1 > 100

- 1 < 100

If you read through these statements, you should be able to say if each one is true or false for you. Our answers differ for the first two conditions, but hopefully we all agree about the last two!

In Python, we might write these expressions as follows:

```
1   age == 30
2   siblings == 2
3   1 > 100
4   1 < 100
```

Notice we can use the < and > operators just like we do in math. But what's with the double equals sign? Is that a typo? Nope, this symbol is the *equality operator*. Remember that a *single* equals sign (=) already has a purpose—to assign values to variables. In the examples, we're not assigning values, we're *checking* values so we have to use a different operator.

As mentioned, each of these expressions can evaluate to either true or false. "True" and "False" are such important concepts that they are in fact keywords in Python. This new data type is unsurprisingly called the *boolean data type*. Both "boolean expression" and "boolean data type" are commonly shortened to just "boolean," and the context implies which is being referred to.

When Python code is evaluated, boolean expressions are converted to their boolean type. That means that the following expressions are all equivalent:

```
1   1 == 1
2   'abc' == 'abc'
3   True
```

Similarly, these expressions are also all equivalent:

```
1   1 == 0
2   'abc' == 'xyz'
3   False
```

To prove this to yourself, open up a Python shell and type some of these in. Python will evaluate each expression and respond with True or False.

There's one more comparison operator to learn and that is the "does not equal" operator. In Python, this is written !=. Try out these expressions in the Python interpreter

```
>>> 1 != 0
>>> True != True
>>> 'abc' != 'xyz'
```

To summarize, here are the operators we know so far, plus >= and <=:

Operator	Type	Purpose
=	Assignment	Assigns a value to a variable
==	Comparison	Checks if two values are equal
!=	Comparison	Checks if two values are not equal
>	Comparison	Checks if the value on the left is greater than the value on the right
>=	Comparison	Checks if the value on the left is greater than or equal to the value on the right
<	Comparison	Checks if the value on the left is less than the value on the right
<=	Comparison	Checks if the value on the left is less than or equal to the value on the right

If-statements

Now that we know about boolean expressions and data types, we can start adding conditions to our code with *if-statements*. An if-statement must have a condition, an action to take if the condition is true, and *optionally* an action to take if the condition is not true. For example:

```
1   n = 50
2   if n < 100:
3       print("The condition is true!")
4   else: # <-- This part is optional
5       print ("The condition is false!")
```

Sometimes it's helpful to put notes for ourselves and others directly into code. These are called *code comments* and they are ignored by Python when the program runs. In Python, code comments start with #.

We can also stack if-statements using the elif keyword:

```
1   n = 150
2   if n < 100:
3       print("n is less than 100.")
4   elif n < 1000:
5       print("n is less than 1000.")
6   else:
7       print("n is a big number!")
```

In Python, elif is the way of writing "else if". It's shortened to elif since it is used so commonly.

Now go ahead and open game.py and change the code as follows:

```
1   print("Escape from Cave Terror!")
2   action_input = input('Action: ')
3   if action_input == 'n':
4       print("Go North!")
5   elif action_input == 's':
6       print("Go South!")
7   elif action_input == 'e':
8       print("Go East!")
9   elif action_input == 'w':
10      print("Go West!")
11  else:
12      print("Invalid action!")
```

This code will read in the user input and compare the value of the input to a predefined character ("n", "s", "e", or "w"). If one of those conditions is true, the program will branch to that part of the code and print the action to the console. Otherwise, it will notify the user that the action is invalid.

Boolean Operations

Sometimes, it is helpful to combine multiple conditions into one, and we do this using the keywords and and or. These work just like you would expect.

```
1    if a == 3 and b == 4:
2        print("The hypotenuse is 5.")
3    if a == 3 or b == 4:
4        print("The hypotenuse might be 5.")
```

You can use as many of these as you need, but when you start combining operators, you sometimes need to include parentheses to specify the order in which the conditions evaluate. Try typing these into the interpreter:

```
>>> 1 == 100 and 1 == 2 or 1 == 1
>>> (1 == 100 and 1 == 2) or 1 == 1
>>> 1 == 100 and (1 == 2 or 1 == 1)
```

The first example is syntactically correct, but confusing to read. To clarify it, in the second example we wrap parentheses around the first two conditions. In the third example, we actually change the order in which the expressions are evaluated so that the response changes.

Here's the difference between the two groupings:

```
1   (1 == 100 and 1 == 2) or 1 == 1
2   (False) or 1 == 1
3   False or True
4   True
```

vs.

```
1   1 == 100 and (1 == 2 or 1 == 1)
2   1 == 100 and (True)
3   False and True
4   False
```

With that in mind, we can do something like this:

```
1   if (a == 3 and b == 4) or (a == 4 and b == 3):
2       print("The hypotenuse is 5.")
```

Note that we cannot do this:

```
1   # Warning: Bad Code!
2   favorite_color = 'blue'
3   if (favorite_color = 'red' or 'orange'):
4       print("You like warm colors.")
```

While the code may make sense when reading it in your head, that is invalid syntax. The statements on either side of an or or and must be complete boolean expressions.

To make our game more user-friendly, let's make each of the conditions ignore the case of the action:

```
1   print("Escape from Cave Terror!")
2   action_input = input('Action: ')
3   if action_input == 'n' or action_input == 'N':
4       print("Go North!")
```

```
5    elif action_input == 's' or action_input == 'S':
6        print("Go South!")
7    elif action_input == 'e' or action_input == 'E':
8        print("Go East!")
9    elif action_input == 'w' or action_input == 'W':
10       print("Go West!")
11   else:
12       print("Invalid action!")
```

If you test the game now, you can verify that actions are accepted regardless of case.

Homework

Try the following exercises for homework:

1. What is the difference between = and ==?

2. Create ages.py to ask the users their age and then print out some information related to their age. For example, if that person is an adult, if they can buy alcohol, they can vote, etc. Note: The int() function can convert a string to an integer.

CHAPTER 5

Functions

In computer programming, a *function* is a named block of code.
Sometimes, values are passed into a function. We have already seen an
example of a function:

```python
print("Hello, World!")
```

The word `print` refers to a block of code inside of the Python core
and we pass it a value to display on the console. If you did the homework
from the last chapter, you also probably used `int()`, which is another
function in the Python core that accepts a value and converts that value
to an integer. Visually, you know something is a function because of the
parentheses. Can you think of another function we've used?

Very similar to a function is a *method*. In fact, functions and methods
are so similar that you will often see the terms used interchangeably. The
difference is, a method is a function that is associated with an object. We'll
talk more about objects later, but for now think of an object as a concrete
"thing" in your application—a person's name, a calendar date, or a favorite
color. An `if` statement is not an object, the `>=` operator is not an object, etc.
An example of a method is the `title()` function that works on strings. Try
this out in the Python shell:

```python
>>> place = "white house"
>>> important_place = place.title()
>>> print(important_place)
```

© Phillip Johnson 2018
P. Johnson, *Make Your Own Python Text Adventure*,
https://doi.org/10.1007/978-1-4842-3231-6_5

You should see that "white house" becomes capitalized to "White House" when you print it out. We can see that `title()` is a *method* because we needed an object (in this case the string "white house") to exist before we could use it. A method is referenced by using the . character. In some ways, you can think of this like the possessive "'s" in English: `place.title()` becomes "place's title function" or "the title function that belongs to the place object".

Data In, Data Out

Most functions **return** a value. For example, the `int()` function gives us back the integer result of whatever we pass in, and the `title()` method gives us a capitalized version of the string. Other functions just "do something" such as the `print()` function. It accepts a value and displays the text, but it doesn't actually give any data back. In practice, we usually take the result of a function that returns something and store it in a variable, whereas we do not do the same with a function like `print()`.

```
1    my_number = '15'
2    # The int() function gives something back, so we save it.
3    my_integer = int(my_number)
4
5    # But this doesn't make sense because print() doesn't give
     anything back.
6    useless_variable = print(my_integer)
```

Of course, we don't always use Python's built-in functions; we often write our own. Remember that a function is a named block of code and the way we name a function is with the `def` keyword. Here is a function that prints a greeting:

```
1    def say_hello():
2    print("Hello, World!")
```

To use that function, we need to call it by writing its name wherever we want the function to run. Create hello.py as follows:

hello.py

```
1   def say_hello():
2   print("Hello, World!")
3
4   say_hello()
5
6   answer = input("Would you like another greeting?")
7   if answer == 'y':
8   say_hello()
```

Each time the program sees say_hello(), it jumps to that block of code and does everything inside of it. Try out this program and verify that "Hello, World!" is always printed out at least once, and that it is optionally printed a second time depending on how you answer.

The say_hello() function does not accept data. We say that this function does not have any *parameters*. A function that *does* accept data must have one or more parameters.[1] Let's try a modified version of say_hello:

```
1 def say_hello(name):
2 print("Hello, " + name)
```

This function has one parameter called name. When the function runs, name actually becomes a variable with the value of whatever was passed in. The function (and *only* the function) can then use the variable wherever it needs to. In this example, the variable is used in order to display the value of the variable in the console.

---

[1]Functions can have up to 255 parameters. Please don't write a function with 255 parameters!

This function also used the + operator to combine or *concatenate* strings into one string. We've now seen that the + operator can be used with numbers in math equations or with strings.

Create hello_name.py to get some practice writing parameterized functions.

hello_name.py

```
1   def say_hello(name):
2       print("Hello, " + name)
3
4   user_name = input("What is your name? ")
5
6   say_hello(user_name)
```

Now that we know about functions, we can organize our game code. Switch back to game.py and create a function that returns the player action.

```
1   def get_player_command():
2       return input('Action: ')
```

Then call this new function in the code that controls player movement.

```
1   print("Escape from Cave Terror!")
2   action_input = get_player_command()
```

Next, indent the code controlling the player movement and wrap it inside of a function. To save space, I don't include the whole function.

```
1   def play():
2       print("Escape from Cave Terror!")
3       action_input = get_player_command()
4       # Remaining code omitted for brevity
```

In order to make the game still playable, at the bottom of the file, make a simple call to the play() function. Here's what your game.py file should look like now:

game.py

```
1   def play():
2       print("Escape from Cave Terror!")
3       action_input = get_player_command()
4       if action_input == 'n' or action_input == 'N':
5           print("Go North!")
6       elif action_input == 's' or action_input == 'S':
7           print("Go South!")
8       elif action_input == 'e' or action_input == 'E':
9           print("Go East!")
10      elif action_input == 'w' or action_input == 'W':
11          print("Go West!")
12      else:
13          print("Invalid action!")
14
15
16  def get_player_command():
17      return input('Action: ')
18
19
20  play()
```

From the user's perspective, the game is unchanged from the previous chapter. But from a coding perspective, we've added some structure to make the code more maintainable. The way code is organized into functions is one of many factors that can make for really nice or really ugly code. As you read and write more code, you will get a better feel for how your own code should be organized.

There is much more that can be said about functions and indeed the entire paradigm of *functional programming* dives deep into functions. Be sure you understand the concepts introduced in this chapter because the rest of the book heavily relies on them.

Homework

Try the following for homework:

1. What keyword is used to create a function?

2. What are some differences between parameterless and parameterized functions?

3. When reading the code for a function, how do you know if it just "does something" or "gives something back"?

4. Create doubler.py to contain one function named double that accepts a single parameter. The function should return the input value multiplied by two. Print out the doubled value of 12345 and 1.57.

5. Create calculator.py to contain one function named add that accepts two parameters. The function should return the sum of the two numbers. Print out the sum of 45 and 55.

6. Create user_calculator.py and re-use your add function from the previous exercise. This time, ask the user for two numbers and print the sum of those numbers. Hint: It is okay if this works only with integers.

CHAPTER 6

Lists

Until now, we have worked with variables that contain only one value, such as age = 30 and name = 'Joe'. But in the real world (and by extension, computer programs), it is often useful to group values together. Consider a program that needs to display the names of all of the students in a class. This would be really annoying to code:

```
1    student1 = 'John'
2    student2 = 'Jack'
3    student3 = 'Ashton'
4    student4 = 'Loretta'
5    print(student1)
6    print(student2)
7    print(student3)
8    print(student4)
```

Imagine a class with 30 or 300 students! In this chapter, we learn how to group these values together and allow them to exist as a group in code.

What Is a List?

When values are grouped together into one variable, it is called a *collection* and a *list* is the most common type of collection used. In Python, a list is created with brackets and commas, as in this example:

```
students = ['John', 'Jack', 'Ashton', 'Loretta']
```

© Phillip Johnson 2018
P. Johnson, *Make Your Own Python Text Adventure*,
https://doi.org/10.1007/978-1-4842-3231-6_6

This is very handy. We can now write code that generically works on all of the students at once. A simplified (although not identical[1]) version of this short program is simply:

```
1    students = ['John', 'Jack', 'Ashton', 'Loretta']
2    print(students)
```

There are two defining characteristics of a list:

- It is *ordered*. The sequence in which things are added to a list is preserved.

- It may contain duplicates.

This means that these two lists are not identical:

```
1    list1 = ['John', 'Jack', 'Ashton', 'Loretta']
2    list2 = ['Ashton', 'Jack', 'John', 'Loretta']
```

And that this list is perfectly okay:

```
list1 = ['Buffalo', 'Buffalo', 'Buffalo', 'Buffalo', 'Buffalo']
```

These characteristics may seem obvious, but we will learn about other collection types later that are unordered and/or do not contain duplicates.

In addition to being able to write code that acts on a list as a whole, Python also provides a lot of handy methods for working with lists.

---

[1]After learning about loops in the next chapter, we could make an identically behaving program.

34

Common List Operations
Add

To add an item to a list, use the append function.

```
>>> my_list = ['A','B','C']
>>> my_list.append('D')
>>> my_list
['A', 'B', 'C', 'D']
```

Length

To find out the length or size of a list, we use the built-in len() function.

```
>>> my_list = ['A','B','C']
>>> len(my_list)
3
>>> my_list.append('D')
>>> len(my_list)
4
```

You may be wondering, why do we write my_list.append() but not my_list.len()? The reason is len() can actually be used with things other than lists, so it lives outside of the List class. Try these in the interpreter:

```
>>> len('Hello, World!')
>>> len({})
```

The first is a string and second is an (empty) dictionary, which is another collection we'll learn about later.

Get

To get a specific item out of a list, you need to know where in the list the item exists. The position of an item in a list is also called the *index*. If we look at the list ['A', 'B', 'C', 'D'], these are how the items are indexed.

index	0	1	2	3
item	A	B	C	D

Note that the indexing starts at 0. Most computer programming languages are 0-indexed, which means that the counting starts at 0.

To get the first item in the list, we use the index 0 as such:

```
>>> my_list = ['A', 'B', 'C', 'D']
>>> my_list[0]
A
```

Be sure to use square brackets when specifying a list index and not parentheses.

To get the last item in the list, we can use the len() function to help:

```
>>> my_list = ['A', 'B', 'C', 'D']
>>> last_position = len(my_list) - 1
>>> my_list[last_position]
D
```

Search

There are two easy ways to search a list for an item. The first will tell us if an item is in a list and the second will tell us *where* an item is in a list.

If you think back to the chapter about if-statements, you learned about boolean operators such as == and <. There's a special boolean operator that can be used with lists, which is simply the word in. Here's how the in operator is used:

```
>>> 2 in [1, 2, 3]
True
>>> 5 in [1, 2, 3]
False
>>> 'A' in ['A', 'B', 'C']
True
```

Sometimes, it is useful to know where the item is in a list. For that, we use the index() function.

```
>>> my_list = ['John', 'Jack', 'Ashton', 'Loretta']
>>> my_list.index('Ashton')
2
```

If an item occurs more than once, the *first* index is returned.

```
>>> my_list = ['Buffalo', 'Buffalo', 'Buffalo']
>>> my_list.index('Buffalo')
0
```

And if an item does not occur in the list, an error is thrown.

```
>>> my_list = ['John', 'Jack', 'Ashton', 'Loretta']
>>> my_list.index('Buffalo')
Traceback (most recent call last):
  File "<stdin>", line 1, in <module>
ValueError: 'Buffalo' is not in list
```

There are other helpful list operations that you can read about in the Python documentation[2].

---

[2]https://docs.python.org/3.5/tutorial/datastructures.html#more-on-lists

Adding Lists to the Game

Now that we know about lists, we can provide the player with a list of items in their inventory. At the top of the play function, add this list:

```
1   def play():
2       inventory = ['Dagger','Gold(5)','Crusty Bread']
```

✎ **Customization Point**   You can change player's inventory by adding, changing, or removing items.

We should also allow the player to view the inventory, so let's make the i key print the inventory. Add this right below the "Go West" action:

```
13  elif action_input == 'i' or action_input == 'I':
14      print("Inventory:")
15      print(inventory)
```

Run the game and verify that you can print the inventory.

We also now have the opportunity to make our code a little cleaner by putting equivalent actions (e.g., 'W' and 'w') into a list. Update your if-statements in the play function as follows:

```
5   if action_input in ['n', 'N']:
6       print("Go North!")
7   elif action_input in ['s', 'S']:
8       print("Go South!")
9   elif action_input in ['e', 'E']:
10      print("Go East!")
11  elif action_input in ['w', 'W']:
12      print("Go West!")
```

```
13   elif action_input in ['i', 'I']:
14       print("Inventory:")
15       print(inventory)
```

This is a personal preference, but I find that easier to read than the previous version. Using a list also allows us to easily add characters in a much less verbose manner. For example, if we wanted to, we could make > an alias for "Go East" by simply adding it to the list: action_input in ['e', 'E', '>'].

Homework

Try the following for homework:

1. What two characteristics make a collection a list?

2. Write code that allows users to enter their three favorite foods. Store those foods in a list.

3. Print out the middle item of this list using an index: ['Mercury', 'Venus', 'Earth']. Could you change your code to work with a list of any size (assuming there are an odd number of items)? Hint: Think back to the int() function that converts something into an integer.

4. What happens when you run this code? Do you know why?

    ```
    >>> my_list = ['A','B','C']
    >>> my_list[len(my_list)]
    ```

CHAPTER 7

Loops

```
All work and no play makes Jack a dull boy

All work and no play makes Jack a dull boy

All work and no play makes Jack a dull boy

All work and no play makes Jack a dull boy
```

The real power of computers is in their ability to execute repetitive tasks without complaint. A CPU is perfectly happy chugging along flipping bits until it burns out. A calculator will keep calculating for as long as you give it numbers to work with. And sure—keep mashing F5 on your favorite web site that is currently having server trouble—your router won't care.

When we want a computer program to run the same piece of code multiple times, we wrap that code inside of a *loop*.

While Loops

Different programming languages have different kinds of loops, but for the most part there are two main categories: "Do something until I say stop" loops and "Do something N number of times" loops. Usually, these are called *while loops* and *for loops*, respectively. Python has one of each kind: a while loop and a for-each loop.

© Phillip Johnson 2018
P. Johnson, *Make Your Own Python Text Adventure*,
https://doi.org/10.1007/978-1-4842-3231-6_7

As it turns out, the only loop you really need is a while loop. However, many programming languages provide other looping keywords to make writing loops easier.

A while loop is always paired with a boolean expression. Remember, boolean expressions are things that can evaluate to true or false. The loop will continue to run *while* the condition is true, hence the name. The while loop in Python is written using the while keyword. Here is an example:

```
1  while True:
2  print("All work and no play makes Jack a dull boy")
```

Try creating a script with that code and run it. Just be ready to press Ctrl+C! You should see that the text flies by as "All work and no play makes Jack a dull boy" is printed out to the console. If left alone, this code would run until the computer shuts down because the boolean expression True is obviously always true.

Let's take a look at a more realistic program. Building on the program from last chapter's homework (you should do that now if you haven't!), what if we wanted the user to keep entering favorite things until they were done? We have no idea if they want to enter one, two, or 20 things, so we use a while loop to keep accepting items. Change the code in favorites.py as follows:

```
1  favorites = []
2  more_items = True
3  while more_items:
4      user_input = input("Enter something you like: ")
5      if user_input == '':
6          more_items = False
```

```
7        else:
8            favorites.append(user_input)
9
10   print("Here are all the things you like!")
11   print(favorites)
```

The first line creates an empty list. Each time the loop runs, another item is added to the list. The boolean condition in the loop is simply more_items, which means in order for the loop to exit, more_items needs to be false. We also could have written while more_items == True, but that is needlessly verbose. To stop adding items, the user should enter an empty string, which can be done by just pressing Enter. Go ahead and run this script and see what the output looks like. Here's what I ended up with:

```
Here are all the things you like!
['family', 'pizza', 'python!']
```

Hmm, looks pretty good, but Python's default behavior for printing lists isn't very pretty. It would be nice if we had some more control over how the list is printed...

For-Each Loops

To start with, let's try to print a bulleted list of all of the favorite items. To do that, we will use a for-each loop. A for-each loop gets its name because it does something for *each* thing in a collection. This is perfect because we want to print each thing in the favorites list. Let's add a function to the top of the file that will pretty print an ordered list for a given collection.

```
1    def pretty_print_unordered(to_print):
2        for item in to_print:
3            print("* " + str(item))
```

The Python syntax for for-each loops is very readable: **for** variable **in** collection. The name of the variable is up to us. Each time the loop runs, the variable points to the next item in the collection. The loop stops running when it reaches the end of the collection.

Inside of the loop, we have access to the current item via the variable defined in the loop syntax. In order to make sure we can print the current item, the variable item is wrapped inside of the str() function to force the item to a string. This function works just like the int() function that you have used before. If we didn't use this, Python could throw an error if a non-string item is encountered.

To use the pretty print function, change the end of the script and rerun it.

```
14    print("Here are all the things you like!")
15    pretty_print_unordered(favorites)
```

You should now see something like this:

```
Here are all the things you like!
* family
* pizza
* python!
```

All right, but what if we want an ordered list with numbers? There's actually a few different ways to do this and we'll go over three of them.

Loop Counters

If we want to print a number for each item, we need to have some way to keep track of *both* an increasing number and the actual item in the loop. The first way we can do that is with a counter.

```
1    def pretty_print_ordered(to_print):
2        i = 1
3        for item in to_print:
```

```
4        print(i + ". " + str(item))
5        i = i + 1
```

In this loop, we set i equal to 1 and each time the loop runs, we increment i by one.[1] The downside to this style is that it requires two extra lines of code and we have to keep track of and update our counter. Another option is to use Python's range() function.

Ranges

Open a Python shell and try out these:

```
>>> list(range(5))
>>> list(range(3,7))
>>> list(range(7,3))
>>> list(range(-2,2))
```

The list() function forces the range into a list that we can easily read. Are you noticing a pattern with int(), str(), and list()?

Using range() gives us a collection of numbers. And we know that a for-each loop can operate on a collection. With that information, we can change our ordered list as follows:

```
1   def pretty_print_ordered(to_print):
2       for i in range(len(to_print)):
3           print(str(i + 1) + ". " + str(to_print[i]))
```

---

[1]It is a convention to use variable i in loops that have a counter; this is one of the few exceptions where it is okay to not use a descriptive variable name!

45

Here, we use the len() function again to get the size of the list and that number gets passed into range() to give a list of numbers that correspond to the indices of the items in the to_print collection. This may seem a little confusing, so let's look at an example:

```
>>> to_print = ['abc', 'def', 'ghi']
>>> len(to_print)
3
>>> list(range(len(to_print)))
[0, 1, 2]
```

In this example, there are three things in the list. Therefore, the range we get back has three numbers: 0, 1, and 2.

Why do we have to use list() in the shell but not in a script? The answer is that range() actually returns a Python range object, not a list object. When a script runs, Python knows how to use the range object. However, when we want to look at the object in the REPL, we need force it to be a list so we can see the values all at once. Using print(range(3)) will print out the unhelpful string "range(3)".

When the loop runs, we use the number from the range function to locate the item in the list at the current index. For example, str(to_print[2]) would return the item in the to_print collection at index 2. Finally, to make the printout user-friendly, we add one to each index in str(i + 1). If we did not do that, we would get a list like this:

```
0. abc
1. def
2. xyz
```

It's correct, but not very user-friendly. Using range() may seem a lot more confusing than using a counter, but the code is shorter and it saves us the trouble of maintaining the counter. The last option we'll learn about is a nice middle ground between the two options we've already seen.

Using Enumerate

Lists are great when we want to store a lot of similar things in one variable, like classroom students. But sometimes we have just two or three[2] variables that are closely associated with each other. In this scenario, a list may be overkill, so instead we use a *tuple*. Like a list, the things in a tuple are ordered and may be duplicated, but *unlike* a list, a tuple's length is fixed. We cannot add or remove items from a tuple. Here are a few situations in which a tuple could make sense:

```
1    first_name, last_name = ('Barack', 'Obama')
2    month, day, year = (10, 22, 2015)
3    dna_aminos = ('A','T','C','G')
```

The tuple syntax allows you to define your variable names on the left and the values on the right. If the number of variables and values match, then each variable is assigned the next value as it appears in the tuple. So in the previous example, month is equal to 10. If just one variable name is used, the whole tuple is assigned to that variable. The value of dna_aminos is ('A','T','C','G') all together.

---

[2]You can actually store a really huge number of items in a tuple, but if you need more than a few variables, you should rethink your choice to use a tuple.

Functions can return tuples too. Try these three different scripts:

```
1   def get_date():
2       return (10, 22, 2015)
3
4   month, day, year = get_date()
5   print(month)
```

```
1   def get_date():
2       return (10, 22, 2015)
3
4   date = get_date()
5   print(date)
```

```
1   def get_date():
2       return (10, 22, 2015)
3
4   month, day = get_date()
5   print(month)
```

The first script works like expected: we *unpack* the tuple returned in the function into month, day, and year. The second script does not unpack the tuple and instead stores all of the parts in the date variable. The last script throws an error because the tuple returned has three values, but we only used two variables. So why the diversion into tuples? Well, the next built-in function we will learn about returns a tuple!

If you pass a collection to the enumerate() function, you will get back a special Python object[3] that behaves like a list of tuples. Each tuple contains two values: the current index and the value from the original list. Try running this code:

---

[3]The object is called an *iterator* if you want to research more. The range() function also returns an iterator.

```
>>> letters = ['a', 'b', 'c']
>>> list(enumerate(letters))
[(0, 'a'), (1, 'b'), (2, 'c')]
>>> list(enumerate(letters, 1))
[(1, 'a'), (2, 'b'), (3, 'c')]
```

So how can we use that to our advantage? Well, in the loop to print things, we could enumerate over the list.

```
1   def pretty_print_ordered(to_print):
2       for i, value in enumerate(to_print, 1):
3           print(str(i) + ". " + str(value))
```

In the for loop, we unpack the tuple into the index i, and we unpack the favorite thing from the list into the variable value. Now that we already have the list value, we don't have to extract it from the list like we did with the range() function. We also don't have to know how long the list is using len()—the enumerator takes care of that for us.

So which is best? As with many things in programming, there isn't one correct answer. In different situations, you could make an argument that any of these is the best solution. For my money, I prefer enumerator in this example. It only takes a few lines of code and is slightly easier to read than the range option. Do you agree? If not, what do you prefer about your choice?

Nesting

A final concept to introduce about loops is *nesting*. A nested loop is simply a loop inside of another loop. Here is a very simple nested loop that creates a small list of multiplication problems.

```
1    for i in range(3):
2        for j in range(3):
3            product = i * j
4            print(str(i) + " * " + str(j) + " = " +
             str(product))
```

Notice that inside of the second loop, we have access to the index from the first loop.[4] In fact the second loop has access to any variables declared between the first loop and second loop.

Suppose we wanted to find the factors of a range of numbers. This would require us to have a different list of factors for each number. Using what we just learned, we can write this script to find the factors for each number from 1 to 10.

```
1    for i in range(1,11):
2        factors = []
3        for j in range(1, i + 1):
4            if i % j == 0:
5                factors.append(j)
6        print("The factors of " + str(i) + " are: " +
         str(factors))
```

The % operator is called the **modulo** or **modulus** operator and it returns the remainder after dividing two numbers. If a % b returns 0, then a is evenly divisible by b as in 4 % 2. This has some handy uses such as doing something every nth time a loop runs. We won't use it much, but it's a good tool to keep in your bag of computer programming tricks.

---

[4]Just like using i is a convention, j is a convention in a nested loop. If you really need them, k and l are next.

This code can access the `factors` list from inside the second loop even though the variable is declared in the first loop.

The Game Loop

In games, most of the code runs inside what is called the *game loop*. Each time the loop runs, the game world changes and user input is passed back into the program. In a 3D game, this may happen 60 times per second! In our game, the loop does not need to run that fast because there are no graphics to redraw. However, the world will be updated and user input will be accepted each time the loop runs.

Add this loop inside of the `play()` function of the game and be sure to indent the rest of the function:

```
1   def play():
2       inventory = ['Dagger','Gold(5)','Crusty Bread']
3       print("Escape from Cave Terror!")
4       while True:
5           action_input = get_player_command()
6           if action_input in ['n', 'N']:
```

Why was a `while` loop used instead of a `for-each` loop? Well, we don't know how many times the loop will run. For now, it runs infinitely, but even in the real game we will need the loop to run until the player wins or loses. Since we don't know how many turns the player will take, we use a `while` loop.

Now that we know how to pretty print a list, let's modify the code that prints the inventory.

```
14  elif action_input in ['i', 'I']:
15      print("Inventory:")
16      for item in inventory:
17          print('*' + str(item))
```

If you run the game now, you'll see that the while loop allows you to keep entering commands and the for loop prints the inventory in a nicer format. To quit the game, use Ctrl+D or Ctrl+C.

Homework

Try the following for homework:

1. What kind of loop would you use for each of the following:

   A. A program that checks the temperature every five seconds

   B. A program that prints receipts at grocery stores

   C. A program that tallies the score in a bowling game

   D. A program that randomly shuffles and plays songs from a music library

2. Open user_calculator.py from Chapter 5 on functions and add a while loop that allows the user to keep adding two numbers.

3. Write a script that displays a multiplication table from 1 * 1 to 10 * 10. Here is what the top-left corner should look like:

   ```
   1 2 3 4
   2 4 6 8
   3 6 9 12
   4 8 12 16
   ```

4. Use enumerate and the % operator to print every third word in this list:

   ```
   ['alpha','beta','gamma','delta','epsilon','zeta','eta']
   ```

CHAPTER 8

Objects

In a computer program, an *object* is a container stored in the computer's memory that holds one or more values. More simply, objects are the "things" available in the program. We have already seen some objects: a string like "Hello, World!" is an object, the list [1, 2, 3] is an object, and even the function print() is an object! In fact, in Python, everything is an object behind the scenes. But most of the time we're actually most interested in the objects we create. By the end of this chapter, you will be able to add objects into your game to represent weapons.

Object Members

In code, objects are often used as the means to bundle related pieces of data. For example, a Person object may contain a string for the person's name, a number for their age, and a list of their favorite foods. Objects can also have their own functions, called *methods*. These methods typically work with the data stored inside the object. Our Person object could have a method that calculates the year the person was born based on their age. Collectively, the data and methods of an object are called the *members* or *properties* of the object.

© Phillip Johnson 2018
P. Johnson, *Make Your Own Python Text Adventure*,
https://doi.org/10.1007/978-1-4842-3231-6_8

Defining Objects with Classes

Before we can create an object, we need to create a *class* to define the object. You can think of a class like a blueprint—it tells us how to *make* a house but it is not a house. We can also reuse the same blueprint to make many similar houses, even if the houses vary in their location, color, etc. To define a class, we use the `class` keyword followed by the name of the class, which is TitleCased by convention.

Create `census.py` and add this class[1]:

```
1   class Person:
2       age = 15
3       name = "Rolf"
4       favorite_foods = ['beets', 'turnips', 'weisswurst']
5
6       def birth_year():
7           return 2015 - age
```

Now, let's add some functionality to our census by creating some people and finding the average age. To create a new object, simply add parentheses after the class name. This code will create three people:

```
1   people = [Person(), Person(), Person()]
2
3   sum = 0
4   for person in people:
5       sum = sum + person.age
6
7   print("The average age is: " + str(sum / len(people)))
```

---

[1]In a real application, we would of course use Python's date and time library to calculate the year born, but this will serve for our demo.

Notice that to access the data in an object, we use the . operator just like we do when accessing a function. The code list.append() is very similar to person.age because append() is a member of the List class and age is a member of the Person class. Running this program should, unsurprisingly, tell us that the average age is 15. What we really need is the ability for each object or *instance* of the Person class to have *different* values for age, name, and favorite foods. To do that, we'll learn about a special function that can be added to any Python object, called __init__().

Using __init()__ to Initialize Objects

In the previous example, we created three identical people. But the Person class is only useful if we can use it to create three people with different names and ages. One option would be something like this:

```
 1    people = [Person(), Person(), Person()]
 2
 3    people[0].name = "Ed"
 4    people[0].age = "11"
 5    people[0].favorite_foods = ["hotdogs", "jawbreakers"]
 6    people[1].name = "Edd"
 7    people[1].age = "11"
 8    people[1].favorite_foods = ["broccoli"]
 9    people[2].name = "Eddy"
10    people[2].age = "12"
11    people[2].favorite_foods = ["chunky puffs", "jawbreakers"]
```

But that is rather verbose and tedious. To ease object creation, Python defines some special behavior around a method named __init__(). First, that method runs immediately upon object creation. Second, we can add arguments to the method that then become required arguments when creating the object. Go ahead and modify your Person class to have the following initializer:

```
1   class Person:
2       def __init__(self, name, age, favorite_foods):
3           self.name = name
4           self.age = age
5           self.favorite_foods = favorite_foods
```

The initializer takes the arguments passed in and assigns them to the object that was just created. Readers paying close attention may have noticed the self keyword popping up in the initializer. That keyword[2] is used to refer to the specific object. That means that the age member in the Person class is not some sort of universal "age", rather, it is the age of this *specific* person that the initializer is acting upon. If it helps, whenever you see self, think that the object is referring to it*self*.

Having defined the initializer, we can create people like this:

```
1   people = [Person("Ed", 11, ["hotdogs", "jawbreakers"])
2       , Person("Edd", 11, ["broccoli"])
3       , Person("Eddy", 12, ["chunky puffs", "jawbreakers"])]
```

That's a lot more convenient than having to set each class member explicitly!

As it turns out, we also need to use self anywhere else in the class where members of the object are accessed or manipulated. That means changing the birth_year() function. Here is the modified Person class:

```
1   class Person:
2       def __init__(self, name, age, favorite_foods):
3           self.name = name
```

---

[2]In fact, self is not a reserved keyword, but it is a convention that everyone follows.

```
4            self.age = age
5            self.favorite_foods = favorite_foods
6
7        def birth_year(self):
8            return 2015 - self.age
```

Let's update our census to also output the average year of birth. To do this, we simply call the birth_year() function on each person object. When the function runs, it runs for that *specific* object. We know this because the function refers to itself via the self keyword.

```
18    age_sum = 0
19    year_sum = 0
20    for person in people:
21    age_sum = age_sum + person.age
22    year_sum = year_sum + person.birth_year()
23
24    print("The average age is: " + str(age_sum / len(people)))
25    print("The average birth year is: " + str(int(year_sum /
      len(people))))
```

Some more magic about the self keyword is that Python knows it refers to the object so you don't have to pass it in manually. Something like person.birth_year(person) is unnecessary and actually incorrect.

I also chose to wrap the average year inside of an int() function because the year "2003" makes more sense than "2003.6666666666667".

Using __str__() to Print Objects

Let's suppose we wanted to display the raw information about the people in the census. A naive approach might be something like this:

```
18    print("The people polled in this census were:")
19    print(people)
```

But now when you run the script, you'll see something like this:

```
The average age is: 11.333333333333334
The average birth year is: 2003
The people polled in this census were:
[<__main__.Person object at 0x10135eb00>, <__main__.Person
object at 0x10135eb38>, <__main__.Person object at 0x10135eb70>]
```

Well that's not very helpful at all! What you are seeing is Python's default implementation of printing objects. It tells you what kind of object the thing is, in this case `Person`, and where it is in memory (the memory location will vary from computer to computer). It would be really nice if we could pass a `Person` into `print()` and see the information about the person.

Thankfully, Python provides an easy way to do this. Like the `__init__()` function that Python looks for, there is also a `__str__()` function that Python looks for when printing objects or when converting an object into a string using the `str()` function. This method must return a string. Go ahead and add this method to the `Person` class:

```
10    def __str__(self):
11        return "Name: " + self.name \
12            + " Age: " + str(self.age) \
13            + " Favorite food: " + str(self.favorite_
              foods[0])
```

For readability, we can use backslashes to wrap a string onto multiple lines. All of those strings will be combined into one string for the function to return. And now when you run the script...the same thing happens. Huh.

A quirk in Python when printing containers (like a list) is that the __str__() method is not called for each object in the container.[3] So we need to do it ourselves with a loop.

```
18    for person in people:
19    print(person)
```

Now, if you run the program, you should see this:

```
The average age is: 11.333333333333334
The average birth year is: 2003
The people polled in this census were:
Name: Ed Age: 11 Favorite food: hotdogs
Name: Edd Age: 11 Favorite food: broccoli
Name: Eddy Age: 12 Favorite food: chunky puffs
```

One last thing to make working with __str__() easier is to use the format() method for strings. Using format() saves us from concatenating strings. Here's an alternative way to write the method:

```
10    def __str__(self):
11        return "Name: {} Age: {} Favorite food: {}".format(
12            self.name, self.age, self.favorite_foods[0])
```

The braces {} are used as placeholders and each of the arguments passed to format() is injected into the placeholders in order. This is often easier to read and write when you need to concatenate a bunch of strings. There are also a lot of other things you can do with format() such as pad

---

[3]The method that is searched for is called __repr__(). We're sticking with __str__() here because the purpose of __str__() is to make objects readable. The purpose of __repr__() is to aid in troubleshooting when something goes wrong in an application. In real applications, you may want to also implement __repr__(), but it's beyond the scope of our game.

strings, truncate long decimal numbers, print currency, etc. If you are interested, you can read all about the string formatting "mini-language" in the Python documentation.[4]

Adding Weapons to the Game

Now that we know how to create classes, let's add some to our game to represent weapons. Add the following at the top of game.py:

```
 1  class Rock:
 2      def __init__(self):
 3          self.name = "Rock"
 4          self.description = "A fist-sized rock, suitable for
            bludgeoning."
 5          self.damage = 5
 6
 7      def __str__(self):
 8          return self.name
 9
10  class Dagger:
11      def __init__(self):
12          self.name = "Dagger"
13          self.description = "A small dagger with some rust. " \
14                             "Somewhat more dangerous than a
                               rock."
15          self.damage = 10
16
```

---

[4]https://docs.python.org/3.5/library/string.html#formatspec

```
17        def __str__(self):
18            return self.name
19
20    class RustySword:
21        def __init__(self):
22            self.name = "Rusty sword"
23            self.description = "This sword is showing its age, " \
24                                "but still has some fight in it."
25            self.damage = 20
26
27        def __str__(self):
28            return self.name
```

Having defined an actual Dagger class, we can now update the starting inventory to include a Dagger object instead of just a string that says "Dagger".

```
1    def play():
2        inventory = [Dagger(),'Gold(5)','Crusty Bread']
3        print("Escape from Cave Terror!")
```

✏ Customization Point   Try defining some of your own weapon types, like Crossbow or Axe. Or if your game is set in a sci-fi world, maybe you want to have RayGun and ShockStick. Just make sure to update the player's inventory accordingly.

What do you think will happen when the players choose to display their inventory? Try it out and see if you were correct!

A Dash of Object-Oriented Programming

In computer programming, a principle that we should strive to follow is "Don't repeat yourself!" or "DRY". If you find yourself typing the same code more than once, there's probably a better way to organize your code. You may have noticed that for each weapon, the __str__() method is exactly the same. Now suppose we wanted to change that method. We would have to make the change in three places. Thankfully, there's a better way.

Object-oriented programming (or OOP) is a paradigm that involves building code around the idea of objects. As mentioned, everything in Python is an object, but we only explicitly started creating objects in this chapter. We were able to do a lot of programming before that because Python supports, but does not require, OOP. In building our game, we'll use some OOP where it helps, but we won't force ourselves into a box unnecessarily just to stick to the paradigm. Structuring the weapons code is one place where OOP can help.

Two important concepts in OOP are *composition* and *inheritance*. Composition is when an object contains another object. We saw this in our census because each Person contained a List of favorite foods. Inheritance is when a class inherits behavior from another class. The metaphor of parent and child applies here and we will sometimes call a class a "parent class" and a class that inherits from the parent a "child class". Alternatively, the terms "superclass" and "subclass" are also used.

To apply inheritance to the weapons, let's start by making a parent class Weapon and move the duplicate __str__() method into the class.

```
1    class Weapon:
2        def __str__(self):
3            return self.name
```

To make a class inherit from Weapon, we use the syntax
ClassName(Weapon):. Any class that inherits from Weapon will
automatically get the same behavior of the Weapon class for free. This
means if we make the Rock, Dagger, and RustySword inherit from Weapon,
we can remove the duplicated __str__() methods.

```python
 6    class Rock(Weapon):
 7        def __init__(self):
 8            self.name = "Rock"
 9            self.description = "A fist-sized rock, suitable for
                  bludgeoning."
10            self.damage = 5
11
12
13    class Dagger(Weapon):
14        def __init__(self):
15            self.name = "Dagger"
16            self.description = "A small dagger with some rust. " \
17                                  "Somewhat more dangerous than a
                                  rock."
18            self.damage = 10
19
20
21    class RustySword (Weapon):
22        def __init__(self):
23            self.name = "Rusty sword"
24            self.description = "This sword is showing its
                  age, " \
25                                  "but still has some fight in it."
26            self.damage = 20
```

Homework

Try the following for homework:

1. What is the difference between a class and an object?

2. What is the purpose of an __init__() method in a class?

3. What is the difference between __str__() and str()?

4. Create a file called food.py that contains a class, Food. This class should have four members: name, carbs, protein, and fat. These members should be set in the initializer of the class.

5. Add a method to the Food class called calories() that calculates the number of calories in the food. There are 4 calories per gram of carbs, 4 calories per gram of protein, and 9 calories per gram of fat.

6. Create another class called Recipe that has an initializer that accepts a name and a list of food items called ingredients. Add a method to this class called calories() that returns the total calories in the recipe.

7. Add a __str__() method to the Recipe class that simply returns the name of the recipe.

8. Create two (simple!) recipes and print out the name and total calories for each recipe. You can make up the numbers for carbs, protein, and fat if you choose. For bonus points, try to do this in a way that would work for two recipes or 200 recipes.

9. The classes in this script are examples of either inheritance or composition. Which one and why?

CHAPTER 9

Exceptions

In a perfect world, programmers never make mistakes and users are always well-behaved. In the real world, programmers always make mistakes and users are never well-behaved! When something goes wrong, Python will raise an *exception,* which is an error encountered while the program is executing. Thankfully, it is possible to handle and recover from most exceptions. In this chapter, we learn about some common exceptions we should anticipate, and how to deal with them.

Validating User Input

Suppose you wanted to collect some basic data about your users and then give them back some information. It seems simple enough:

```
1   name = input("Please enter your name: ")
2   age = input("Please enter your age: ")
3   print("You were born in {}.".format(2015 - int(age)))
```

You test the program and it works perfectly. Then you show it to your friend, and she enters "25 years" for age. Well, this unhelpful message dumps out to the screen and now it looks like you don't know how to program.

```
Traceback (most recent call last):
  File "validate.py", line 3, in <module>
    print("You were born in {}.".format(2015 - int(age)))
ValueError: invalid literal for int() with base 10: '25 years'
```

© Phillip Johnson 2018
P. Johnson, *Make Your Own Python Text Adventure,*
https://doi.org/10.1007/978-1-4842-3231-6_9

This is an exception (specifically a `ValueError`), and it was raised because the user entered a value that could not be converted into a number using `int()`. Being diligent programmers, we can anticipate and plan for this situation.

The keyword `try` allows us to mark a block of code as something that could raise an exception. It is followed by the `except` keyword, which marks the block of code to run should an exception be encountered.

```
1   name = input("Please enter your name: ")
2   age = input("Please enter your age: ")
3   try:
4       print("You were born in {}.".format(2015 - int(age)))
5   except ValueError:
6       print('Unable to calculate the year you were born, ' \
7               + '"{}" is not a number.'.format(age))
```

Pay special attention to the syntax here and remember that whitespace in Python is meaningful. The indentation shows us what code is part of the `try` block and what code is part of the `except` block. If any code inside of the `try` block encounters a `ValueError`, the program will immediately jump to the except block and run the code inside that block.

Checking Object Members

In our game, the player has an inventory of a few assorted items. Let's add one more:

```
inventory = [Rock(), Dagger(), 'Gold(5)', 'Crusty Bread']
```

Some of those are weapons and some are not. If we wanted to find the most powerful weapon in the inventory, we'd need to check each item and see what its damage is.

```
59    def most_powerful_weapon(inventory):
60        max_damage = 0
61        best_weapon = None
62        for item in inventory:
63            if item.damage > max_damage:
64                best_weapon = item
65                max_damage = item.damage
66
67        return best_weapon
```

This should be pretty straight-forward. The function loops over all of the items in the inventory and checks the damage to see if it is greater than what has already been found. There is one new keyword here: None. It is the absence of a value. We set best_weapon equal to None initially because if the player does not have any weapons, the function can't return a weapon!

If you run this code, it unfortunately raises an exception:

```
Traceback (most recent call last):
  File "game.py", line 80, in <module>
    play()
  File "game.py", line 46, in play
    best_weapon = most_powerful_weapon(inventory)
  File "game.py", line 59, in most_powerful_weapon
    if item.damage > max_damage:
AttributeError: 'str' object has no attribute 'damage'
```

This makes sense because "Crusty Bread" and "Gold" don't do damage. Since we know the inventory will often have non-weapons, we can wrap the code in a try and handle the AttributeError.

```
59    def most_powerful_weapon(inventory):
60        max_damage = 0
61        best_weapon = None
```

```
62      for item in inventory:
63          try:
64              if item.damage > max_damage:
65                  best_weapon = item
66                  max_damage = item.damage
67          except AttributeError:
68              pass
69
70      return best_weapon
71
72  play()
```

If an AttributeError is encountered, we don't actually need to do anything because we don't care that Crusty Bread doesn't have a damage attribute. The keyword pass can be used any time we simply want to skip over or ignore a code block. Keep in mind that for most exceptions, you want to do something, such as alert the user or follow a different code path. For this specific situation, we're safe to ignore the exception.

Raising Exceptions Intentionally

It may seem counter-intuitive at first, but there are some scenarios where we actually want to cause an exception to be raised. We usually do this when we want to yell at ourselves for doing something wrong! Putting in checks for bad code will help us catch errors during testing.

One vulnerability in the current code is with the Weapon class. This code would cause an exception:

```
1   axe = Weapon()
2   print(axe)
```

Why? Because the __str__() method of the Weapon class looks for a name when printing the object, but the class doesn't have that attribute. We could fix this by assigning a name to Weapon, but that doesn't really make sense because the class is too general to describe. Really, we should never create a Weapon object; we should always create a specific subclass like Dagger. If we need an axe object, we should create an Axe class that inherits from the superclass Weapon.

To prevent ourselves from accidentally creating Weapon objects, we can raise an exception in the initializer.

```
1   class Weapon:
2       def __init__(self):
3           raise NotImplementedError("Do not create raw Weapon
            objects.")
4
5       def __str__(self):
6           return self.name
```

The NotImplementedError exception is built into Python and it is a good marker to alert us that we're doing something wrong. We can include a message for the exception to help remind us what the problem is. If you would like to test this new code, try adding Weapon() to the player's inventory and running the game. You should see this error:

```
Traceback (most recent call last):
  File "game.py", line 72, in <module>
    play()
  File "game.py", line 33, in play
    inventory = [Weapon(), Rock(), Dagger(), 'Gold(5)',
    'Crusty Bread']
  File "game.py", line 3, in __init__
    raise NotImplementedError("Do not create raw Weapon
    objects.")
NotImplementedError: Do not create raw Weapon objects.
```

Just remember to remove Weapon() from the inventory when you're done testing.

Homework

Try the following for homework:

1. Update user_calculator.py with try and except to handle a user who doesn't enter a number.

2. What does None mean and when is it used?

3. What does pass mean and when is it used?

4. Create a Vehicle class, a Motorcycle class that is a subclass of Vehicle with a wheels attribute set to 2, and a Car class that is a subclass of Vehicle with a wheels attribute set to 4. Add code that will raise an exception if the programmer tries to create a Vehicle.

CHAPTER 10

Intermezzo

Believe it or not, by now you actually know most of the Python material
this book will cover. There will be a few new things to learn, but the rest
of the book will focus on making the game. Along the way, we will pick up
some best practices and guidelines for building applications. To start with,
we're going to reorganize the code into a few files.

Organizing Code Into Multiple Files

First, we're going to create items.py that will store all of the classes for the
items the player will interact with. Right now, we just have weapons, but
later we will add more.

items.py

```
1    class Weapon:
2        def __init__(self):
3            raise NotImplementedError("Do not create raw
             Weapon objects.")
4
5        def __str__(self):
6            return self.name
7
8
9    class Rock(Weapon):
```

© Phillip Johnson 2018
P. Johnson, *Make Your Own Python Text Adventure,*
https://doi.org/10.1007/978-1-4842-3231-6_10

```
10         def __init__(self):
11             self.name = "Rock"
12             self.description = "A fist-sized rock, suitable for
                   bludgeoning."
13             self.damage = 5
14
15
16     class Dagger(Weapon):
17         def __init__(self):
18             self.name = "Dagger"
19             self.description = "A small dagger with some rust. " \
20                                 "Somewhat more dangerous than a
                                 rock."
21             self.damage = 10
22
23
24     class RustySword(Weapon):
25         def __init__(self):
26             self.name = "Rusty sword"
27             self.description = "This sword is showing its age, " \
28                                 "but still has some fight in it."
29             self.damage = 20
```

Next, we will create player.py with a Player class. Since the inventory is really associated with the player, we will make it an attribute of the object. This also means that the methods associated with printing the inventory need to be moved to the Player class. We'll cover import after we're finished reorganizing.

player.py

```
1    import items
2
3
4    class Player:
5        def __init__(self):
6            self.inventory = [items.Rock(),
7                              items.Dagger(),
8                              'Gold(5)',
9                              'Crusty Bread']
10
11       def print_inventory(self):
12           print("Inventory:")
13           for item in self.inventory:
14               print('* ' + str(item))
15           best_weapon = self.most_powerful_weapon()
16           print("Your best weapon is your {}".format
             (best_weapon))
17
18       def most_powerful_weapon(self):
19           max_damage = 0
20           best_weapon = None
21           for item in self.inventory:
22               try:
23                   if item.damage > max_damage:
24                       best_weapon = item
25                       max_damage = item.damage
26               except AttributeError:
27                   pass
28
29           return best_weapon
```

Note that the methods are similar to before, but not identical. Now that we are inside of an object, we need to use self when appropriate.

Finally, we need to clean up our game function to account for these changes.

game.py

```
1    from player import Player
2
3
4    def play():
5        print("Escape from Cave Terror!")
6        player = Player()
7        while True:
8            action_input = get_player_command()
9            if action_input in ['n', 'N']:
10                print("Go North!")
11            elif action_input in ['s', 'S']:
12                print("Go South!")
13            elif action_input in ['e', 'E']:
14                print("Go East!")
15            elif action_input in ['w', 'W']:
16                print("Go West!")
17            elif action_input in ['i', 'I']:
18                player.print_inventory()
19            else:
20                print("Invalid action!")
21
22
23    def get_player_command():
24        return input('Action: ')
25
26
27    play()
```

Importing from Other Files

Since we moved the code into other files (or modules), we need a way for the code to be able to reference those modules. The `import` keyword can be used to pull in objects from other modules. It appears at the top of a Python file.

There are two primary styles:

import module

and

from module import ClassName

The first style gives us access to all of the classes in the referenced module. However, we have to prefix any class from that module with the name of the module. For example, in the player's inventory, we have to write `items.Rock()`, which means the `Rock` class in the `items` module. Had we left it as just `Rock()`, Python would search the `player` module and naturally not find the class.

The second style is typically used when you need just one or two classes from a module. In our game, the `player` module only has one class, so we could use either style. For readability, I prefer `player = Player()` over `player = player.Player()`, so I chose the second `import` style.

Run the game now and verify that the game works the same as before. These changes are an example of *refactoring*. Refactoring is the work we do to improve code quality without affecting the behavior of the code. It's always a good idea to step back and refactor code periodically, otherwise you'll find yourself with a lot of messy code. In the corporate world, we usually call this "legacy" code. No one wants to touch the legacy code.

Although the imports seem to work magically here, that is only because all of the modules are in the directory from which we are running the code. Python searches a few different locations for modules. If you'd like to learn more, you can read about the PYTHONPATH.[1] Otherwise, just keep in mind that you can't drop modules in random locations on the filesystem and expect them to be picked up by Python.

Homework

This time, the homework is review:

1. Go back through the chapters and review anything that you struggled with. Otherwise, take a break and get ready to plunge into world building!

---

[1] https://docs.python.org/3/using/cmdline.html

CHAPTER 11

Building Your World

Early on, we gave our players the ability to move throughout the game world, but so far that world has been only a figment of our imaginations. In this chapter, we will finally create the world for the players to move around in.

The X-Y Grid

Since this is a text adventure, we only need to worry about the players moving in two directions: forward/backward and left/right. This allows us to build the world as if we were looking from above down onto the players, similar to Pac-Man or Chess. To keep track of where everything is, we use a coordinate plane similar to the one you learned about in math class. The X-axis represents the horizontal position of game objects and the Y-axis represents the vertical position of the game objects. However, in game programming, we orient the grid slightly differently.

A typical coordinate plane in math and science looks like this:

```
(0,2)—(1,2)—(2,2)
  |      |      |
(0,1)—(1,1)—(2,1)
  |      |      |
(0,0)—(1,0)—(2,0)
```

But in game programming, we flip the Y-axis so that the numbers increase downward instead of upward.

© Phillip Johnson 2018
P. Johnson, *Make Your Own Python Text Adventure*,
https://doi.org/10.1007/978-1-4842-3231-6_11

```
(0,0)——(1,0)——(2,0)
  |       |       |
(0,1)——(1,1)——(2,1)
  |       |       |
(0,2)——(1,2)——(2,2)
```

If we label the spaces instead of the intersection, we end up with a grid of cells.

(0,0)	(1,0)	(2,0)
(0,1)	(1,1)	(2,1)
(0,2)	(1,2)	(2,2)

We can imagine each grid cell to be a different part of the cave (or room in a spaceship, or city block). Players will be in one cell at any time and in that cell they may encounter an enemy, loot, or some lovely scenery. They can move from cell to cell by using the already defined actions North, South, East, and West. These actions correspond to Up (y - 1), Down (y + 1), Left (x - 1), and Right (x + 1), respectively.

Before we go much further, let's get some of this written up into code. Start by creating a new module called world.py with the following tile classes.

```
1   class MapTile:
2       def __init__(self, x, y):
3           self.x = x
4           self.y = y
5
6       def intro_text(self):
```

```
 7          raise NotImplementedError("Create a subclass
            instead!")
 8
 9
10   class StartTile(MapTile):
11       def intro_text(self):
12           return """
13           You find yourself in a cave with a flickering torch
             on the wall.
14           You can make out four paths, each equally as dark
             and foreboding.
15           """
16
17
18   class BoringTile(MapTile):
19       def intro_text(self):
20           return """
21           This is a very boring part of the cave.
22           """
23
24
25   class VictoryTile(MapTile):
26       def intro_text(self):
27           return """
28           You see a bright light in the distance...
29           ... it grows as you get closer! It's sunlight!
30
31
32           Victory is yours!
```

✏️ **Customization Point**   Change the intro text of the tiles to fit your game world.

The `MapTile` class is the superclass that defines the initializer. The following subclasses are specific types of tiles in the game. (Don't worry, we'll get rid of `BoringTile`!) The `intro_text()` method will be used in the next section, but you should be able to guess its purpose. Notice that we raise an exception if a naughty programmer tries to use `MapTile` directly.

You may have noticed the triple quote (`"""`) surrounding the intro text. Python allows us to write multi-line strings by surrounding text with triple quotes. This can make it easier to write long strings.

Having defined the classes, we need to place them into a grid.

```
35    world_map = [
36         [None,VictoryTile(1,0),None],
37         [None,BoringTile(1,1),None],
38         [BoringTile(0,2),StartTile(1,2),BoringTile(2,2)],
39         [None,BoringTile(1,3),None]
40    ]
```

This list of lists is a way of representing the grid pattern. The "outside" list represents the Y-axis. So, the first item in the "outside" list is the entire first row and the second item in the "outside" list is the entire second row. Each "inside" list represents a single row. The first item in the first row is the tile in the top-left corner in the grid. The last item in the last row is the tile in the bottom-right corner of the grid. The None value is used for the grid spaces where we do not want a map tile to exist.

For convenience, let's also add a function that locates the tile at a coordinate.

```
42    def tile_at(x, y):
43         if x < 0 or y < 0:
44              return None
```

```
45        try:
46              return world_map[y][x]
47        except IndexError:
48              return None
```

The world_map[y][x] syntax may look confusing, but that's because we're working with a list of lists. The world_map[y] part selects the row of the map and adding [x] selects the specific cell in that row. Catching IndexError will handle the situation where we pass in a coordinate greater than the bounds of the map and if x < 0 or y < 0 handles coordinates smaller than the bounds of the map. Without this function, we'd have to continually check the bounds of the world whenever we wanted to see if a tile exists.

Moving in the World

One of the first features we added to the game was getting user input for moving in the game world. However, until now, those have just been placebo actions. To make the players move, we need to add X-Y coordinates to the Player class to represent the player's position, and we need to add methods that modify those coordinates. Start by adding self.x and self.y in the initializer.

```
4     class Player:
5         def __init__(self):
6             self.inventory = [items.Rock(),
7                                  items.Dagger(),
8                                  'Gold(5)',
9                                  'Crusty Bread']
10
11            self.x = 1
12            self.y = 2
```

Next, add these methods inside the class:

```
34   def move(self, dx, dy):
35       self.x += dx
36       self.y += dy
37
38   def move_north(self):
39       self.move(dx=0, dy=-1)
40
41   def move_south(self):
42       self.move(dx=0, dy=1)
43
44   def move_east(self):
45       self.move(dx=1, dy=0)
46
47   def move_west(self):
48       self.move(dx=-1, dy=0)
```

If you didn't read through the homework answers, the syntax move(dx=0, dy=-1) may be new to you. This code calls the move method using *named parameters.* Named parameters are never required, but they can make it easier to read code, especially when you have parameters of the same type in the method. The names dx and dy come from math and mean "change in x" and "change in y," respectively. So the move() method accepts a generic change in the x- and/or y-direction and the specific methods define the amount of the change.

Finally, our main game loop needs to use these methods instead of just printing out the placeholder text. Jump over to game.py and change the play() function as follows.

```
12   if action_input in ['n', 'N']:
13       player.move_north()
14   elif action_input in ['s', 'S']:
```

```
15        player.move_south()
16    elif action_input in ['e', 'E']:
17        player.move_east()
18    elif action_input in ['w', 'W']:
19        player.move_west()
20    elif action_input in ['i', 'I']:
21        player.print_inventory()
```

Now the players will be able to move around in the map, but we should also display the intro text for each tile so the players know where they are. Don't forget to import the world module.

```
1    from player import Player
2    import world
3
4
5    def play():
6        print("Escape from Cave Terror!")
7        player = Player()
8        while True:
9            room = world.tile_at(player.x, player.y)
10           print(room.intro_text())
11           action_input = get_player_command()
```

Help! What's an `AttributeError`?   A very common problem at this point in the game is that you get an error that says `AttributeError: 'NoneType' object has no attribute 'intro_text'`.

What does it mean?   It means that the Python code says to run the `intro_text()` method on an object, but that object is actually the None type.

Why does it happen?   The error occurs when the player moves into a room that doesn't exist. More specifically, when the player moves into a part of the map that is marked None.

How do I fix it?   If the error shows up right away, it probably means the starting location for your player is wrong. Check the __init()__ of the Player class and make sure the self.x and self.y coordinates are correct. Remember to start counting at zero!

If the error shows up while you're moving around, you are moving into a room that doesn't exist. If you want the room to exist, change your map. If you moved there by mistake, you found a bug that we'll fix soon!

You should be able to test the game now and verify that you can move around the world. There's some bugs right now. Notably, the game doesn't end when you reach the VictoryTile and the players can also wrap around the map. We'll fix those bugs, but for now, enjoy the fact that this is starting to feel more like a game!

CHAPTER 12

Making the World More Interesting

With no risk to the player, our game is pretty boring right now. We're going to fix that by adding enemies and making the player vulnerable. But we'll also give the player the ability to fight back and heal so that they have a fighting chance for making it out alive.

Enemies

By now, the pattern of creating a base class with multiple subclasses should look familiar. We'll use that pattern for creating enemies. Each enemy will have a name, hp (health), and damage. Create these enemy classes in a new module called enemies.py.

enemies.py

```
1    class Enemy:
2        def __init__(self):
3            raise NotImplementedError("Do not create raw Enemy
             objects.")
4
5        def __str__(self):
6            return self.name
```

```
7
8       def is_alive(self):
9           return self.hp > 0
10
11
12   class GiantSpider(Enemy):
13       def __init__(self):
14           self.name = "Giant Spider"
15           self.hp = 10
16           self.damage = 2
17
18
19   class Ogre(Enemy):
20       def __init__(self):
21           self.name = "Ogre"
22           self.hp = 30
23           self.damage = 10
24
25
26   class BatColony(Enemy):
27       def __init__(self):
28           self.name = "Colony of bats"
29           self.hp = 100
30           self.damage = 4
31
32
33   class RockMonster(Enemy):
34       def __init__(self):
35           self.name = "Rock Monster"
36           self.hp = 80
37           self.damage = 15
```

Customization Point   You can create your own enemy types, just make sure they all have a name, hp, and damage.

To place enemies into the cave, we'll need a new type of Tile. This tile will need to generate an enemy and the intro text should appropriately state if the enemy is alive or dead. Start by switching over to world.py and add import random to the top of the file. The random module is built into Python and it provides methods for randomly generating numbers.

Since our enemies are not all equally as easy to defeat, we'll want players to encounter them with different frequency. For example, we could have them encounter a Giant Spider about 50% of the time and a Rock Monster only 5% of the time. The random() method in the random module returns a decimal number from 0.0 to 1.0, which means about 50% of the time, the randomly returned number will be less than 0.5.

```
25    class EnemyTile(MapTile):
26        def __init__(self, x, y):
27            r = random.random()
28            if r < 0.50:
29                self.enemy = enemies.GiantSpider()
30            elif r < 0.80:
31                self.enemy = enemies.Ogre()
32            elif r < 0.95:
33                self.enemy = enemies.BatColony()
34            else:
35                self.enemy = enemies.RockMonster()
36
37            super().__init__(x, y)
```

📝 **Customization Point**   Adjust the numbers to make the game easier or harder. A harder game might use 0.40, 0.70, and 0.90, for example. If you have more than four enemy types, make sure you define the percentages for each type.

Each time a new EnemyTile is created, a new enemy will also be created. That enemy will be linked to the tile since we used the self keyword for the enemy variable. The line of code at the bottom of the initializer will take the X-Y coordinates for this tile and pass them to the __init__() method of the superclass, MapTile. We don't have to do this explicitly in StartTile because we did not define an __init()__ method for that class. If an initializer is *not* defined on a subclass, the superclass initializer will be called automatically.

To alert the player about the enemy, we can create the intro_text() method for the EnemyTile class. This method calls the is_alive() method that we defined in the Enemy class.

```
39    def intro_text(self):
40        if self.enemy.is_alive():
41            return "A {} awaits!".format(self.enemy.name)
42        else:
43            return "You've defeated the {}.".format(self.
              enemy.name)
```

Now that we have a more interesting tile, let's delete the BoringTile class and replace any references to the class in the map with EnemyTile.

```
56    world_map = [
57        [None,VictoryTile(1,0),None],
58        [None,EnemyTile(1,1),None],
59        [EnemyTile(0,2),StartTile(1,2),EnemyTile(2,2)],
60        [None,EnemyTile(1,3),None]
61    ]
```

You can play the game now, but you'll recognize that you can't do anything to the enemies and the enemies don't do anything to you. Fixing the first issue is pretty easy: we just need to add an attack method to the Player class, and then let the player initiate that action.

This new method on the Player class will take advantage of the most_powerful_weapon() method we already wrote and then use that weapon against the enemy. Make sure you import world at the top of the class too!

```
71   def attack(self):
72       best_weapon = self.most_powerful_weapon()
73       room = world.tile_at(self.x, self.y)
74       enemy = room.enemy
75       print("You use {} against {}!".format(best_weapon.
         name, enemy.name))
76       enemy.hp -= best_weapon.damage
77       if not enemy.is_alive():
78           print("You killed {}!".format(enemy.name))
79       else:
80           print("{} HP is {}.".format(enemy.name, enemy.hp))
```

To allow the player to use this method, add another elif to the branch in game.py:

```
13   if action_input in ['n', 'N']:
14       player.move_north()
15   elif action_input in ['s', 'S']:
16       player.move_south()
17   elif action_input in ['e', 'E']:
18       player.move_east()
19   elif action_input in ['w', 'W']:
20       player.move_west()
21   elif action_input in ['i', 'I']:
```

```
22        player.print_inventory()
23    elif action_input in ['a', 'A']:
24        player.attack()
```

Since this method automatically chooses the best weapon, I removed the two lines from print_inventory() that display the best weapon to the user. This is optional and has no effect on the gameplay, so you can leave them in if you like, but you'll no longer see those lines in the example code.

Before the enemy is able to attack the player, the Player class needs to have its own hp member. We can add this easily in the initializer:

```
4    class Player:
5        def __init__(self):
6            self.inventory = [items.Rock(),
7                              items.Dagger(),
8                              'Gold(5)',
9                              items.CrustyBread()]
10           self.x = 1
11           self.y = 2
12           self.hp = 100
```

To make the enemy fight back, we need to provide some logic within the EnemyTile class. The EnemyTile class is the part of the game that knows about the strength of the current enemy. Since we might want other tiles to also be able to respond to the player, let's name the method generically as modify_player() so we can reuse the name in other tiles.

```
56   def modify_player(self, player):
57       if self.enemy.is_alive():
58           player.hp = player.hp - self.enemy.damage
59           print("Enemy does {} damage. You have {} HP
                 remaining.".
60                 format(self.enemy.damage, player.hp))
```

We should now call this method from the game loop so that the enemy responds as soon as the player enters the tile. Add this line to the play() method:

```
8    while True:
9        room = world.tile_at(player.x, player.y)
10       print(room.intro_text())
11       room.modify_player(player) # New line
12       action_input = get_player_command()
```

Notice that this method gets called every time, regardless of the tile type. But since we've only added the method to the EnemyTile. The game would raise an exception in its current state. One way to fix it would be to add modify_player() to every tile class, but that would violate the DRY principle discussed earlier. A better choice is to add a base implementation in the MapTile class. Remember that any subclass of MapTile will inherit the behavior in MapTile, *unless* it is overridden. We don't really want the base method to do anything, so we can use the pass keyword.

```
1    class MapTile:
2        def __init__(self, x, y):
3            self.x = x
4            self.y = y
5
6        def intro_text(self):
7            raise NotImplementedError("Create a subclass
             instead!")
8
9        def modify_player(self, player):
10           pass
```

Now the game should feel more "real" when you play it. There's some sense of danger because you can take damage, but you also feel in control because you can move and attack when necessary. Indeed, there are still bugs (which we'll fix!), but the core elements of the game are now in place.

I chose to add one final touch, which is to make each tile's intro text a bit more descriptive based on the status of the enemy in the tile. Here's the complete EnemyTile with that enhancement.

```
1   class EnemyTile(MapTile):
2       def __init__(self, x, y):
3           r = random.random()
4           if r < 0.50:
5               self.enemy = enemies.GiantSpider()
6               self.alive_text = "A giant spider jumps down
                                  from " \
7                                 "its web in front of you!"
8               self.dead_text = "The corpse of a dead
                                 spider " \
9                                "rots on the ground."
10          elif r < 0.80:
11              self.enemy = enemies.Ogre()
12              self.alive_text = "An ogre is blocking your
                                  path!"
13              self.dead_text = "A dead ogre reminds you of
                                 your triumph."
14          elif r < 0.95:
15              self.enemy = enemies.BatColony()
16              self.alive_text = "You hear a squeaking noise
                                  growing louder" \
17                                "...suddenly you are lost
                                  in s swarm of bats!"
18              self.dead_text = "Dozens of dead bats are
                                 scattered on the ground."
19          else:
```

```
20              self.enemy = enemies.RockMonster()
21              self.alive_text = "You've disturbed a rock
                                  monster " \
22                                "from his slumber!"
23              self.dead_text = "Defeated, the monster has
                                  reverted " \
24                                "into an ordinary rock."
25
26          super().__init__(x, y)
27
28      def intro_text(self):
29          text = self.alive_text if self.enemy.is_alive()
            else self.dead_text
30          return text
31
32      def modify_player(self, player):
33          if self.enemy.is_alive():
34              player.hp = player.hp - self.enemy.damage
35              print("Enemy does {} damage. You have {} HP
                remaining.".
36                      format(self.enemy.damage, player.hp))
```

✏️ **Customization Point**   Rewrite the intro text for each tile to fit the mood of your game.

Do You Have Any Potions…or Food?

Remember when we gave the player some crusty bread in their inventory? Well, now we'll make it useful. Instead of being just a string, we'll make it into something the player can consume to heal. First, create these two classes in items.py.

```
32    class Consumable:
33        def __init__(self):
34            raise NotImplementedError("Do not create raw
              Consumable objects.")
35
36        def __str__(self):
37            return "{} (+{} HP)".format(self.name, self.
              healing_value)
38
39
40    class CrustyBread(Consumable):
41        def __init__(self):
42            self.name = "Crusty Bread"
43            self.healing_value = 10
```

🖊 **Customization Point**   Add another Consumable type for a food the character could likely encounter in your game world.

The base class allows us to make a new kind of consumable item in the future, such as a healing potion. For now, we just have the one subclass, CrustyBread. We should now change the player's inventory in player.py to have an actual CrustyBread object, instead of the string.

```
1    class Player:
2        def __init__(self):
3            self.inventory = [items.Rock(),
4                              items.Dagger(),
5                              'Gold(5)',
6                              items.CrustyBread()]
```

Next we need to create a heal() function for the player. This function should:

1. Determine what items the player has available to heal with

2. Display those items to the player

3. Take player input to determine the item to use

4. Consume that item and remove it from the inventory

It sounds like a lot, but this actually won't take too many lines of code. To start, we want to find the Consumables in the inventory. Python's built-in function isinstance() accepts an object and a type and tells us if that object is that type or a subclass of that type. In the REPL, isinstance(1, int) is True and isinstance(1, str) is False, because the number one is an int, but not a str (string). Similarly, isinstance(CrustyBread(), Consumable) is True because CrustyBread is a subclass of Consumable, but isinstance(CrustyBread(), Enemy) is False.

Here's one way to use that function:

```
1   consumables = []
2   for item in self.inventory:
3       if isinstance(item, Consumable):
4           consumables.append(item)
```

That's perfectly reasonable and correct, but we can make it a bit more concise using a *list comprehension*. List comprehensions are a special feature in Python that let us create a list "on the fly". The syntax is [what_we_want for thing in iterable if condition]:

*   what_we_want: What ends up in the new list. This is often just the thing in the iterable, but we can modify the thing if we want.

- thing: The object in the iterable.

- iterable: Something that can be passed to a for-each loop, such as a list, range, or tuple.

- condition: (Optional.) A condition to limit what is added to the list.

To help make this concrete, try these comprehensions in the REPL:

- [a for a in range(5)]

- [a*2 for a in range(5)]

- [a for a in range(5) if a > 3]

- [a*2 for a in range(5) if a > 3]

Here's the comprehension we will use to filter the player's inventory:

```
19  def heal(self):
20      consumables = [item for item in self.inventory
21                      if isinstance(item, items.Consumable)]
```

Sometimes, the player won't have anything to eat, so we need to check for that condition. If consumables is an empty list, we should alert the player and exit the heal() method.

```
19  def heal(self):
20      consumables = [item for item in self.inventory
21                      if isinstance(item, items.Consumable)]
22      if not consumables:
23          print("You don't have any items to heal you!")
24          return
```

The if not consumables line is a shortcut that means "if there is nothing in the list" or if consumables == []. If that's the case, we need to exit the function, which we do with return. You've seen return before, but here we're returning...nothing? Exactly! If you need to immediately exit a function, the return keyword by itself will do just that.

Next, we need to find out what the player wants to eat.

```
19   def heal(self):
20       consumables = [item for item in self.inventory
21                           if isinstance(item, items.Consumable)]
22       if not consumables:
23           print("You don't have any items to heal you!")
24           return
25
26       for i, item in enumerate(consumables, 1):
27           print("Choose an item to use to heal: ")
28           print("{}. {}".format(i, item))
29
30       valid = False
31       while not valid:
32           choice = input("")
33           try:
34               to_eat = consumables[int(choice) - 1]
35               self.hp = min(100, self.hp + to_eat.healing_
                 value)
36               self.inventory.remove(to_eat)
37               print("Current HP: {}".format(self.hp))
38               valid = True
39           except (ValueError, IndexError):
40               print("Invalid choice, try again.")
```

The only new thing here is the built-in function min(), which returns the lesser of two values. This caps the player's HP at 100. Other than that, this function is a good review of some concepts we've gone over before. It might behoove you to go through it line-by-line to make sure you understand what each line's purpose is.

Finally, we need to give the player the ability to use this new function. Open game.py and add the lines to let the user heal.

```
25    elif action_input in ['h', 'H']:
26        player.heal()
```

Try the game now and make sure that you can heal as long as you have some crusty bread in your inventory. You should also try to enter a bad value like 5 when asked to make a choice and verify that the code handles that situation appropriately.

We added a lot of new features to the game in this chapter. In the next chapter, we'll take some time to clean up our code and fix some of the bugs.

CHAPTER 13

World-Building Part 2

At this point, we've built a pretty decent game world for the player to move around in and experience. However, along the way, we've introduced some unintentional bugs that need to be resolved. To help fix those bugs, we'll introduce a new data structure called a *dictionary* to help make our code cleaner.

Dictionaries

In real life, a person uses a dictionary to search for a word and retrieve a **definition**. A Python dictionary works on the same principle, except instead of just words, any type of object[1] can be searched for and the "definition" can also be any type of object. Generally, we call this a *key-value pair* where the *key* is what we search by and the *value* is the object linked to that key. A concrete example is a dictionary where the key is the name of the city and the value is the population. We'll use this example to introduce the syntax for working with dictionaries.

---

[1]Actually, only "immutable" objects can be can be used for keys in dictionaries. An immutable object is one that cannot change, such as a string or integer.

© Phillip Johnson 2018
P. Johnson, *Make Your Own Python Text Adventure*,
https://doi.org/10.1007/978-1-4842-3231-6_13

Creating a Dictionary

A dictionary is created using braces { }:

```
>>> cities = {"Amsterdam": 780000, "Brasilia": 2480000,
"Canberra": 360000}
```

Get

To get a value from a dictionary, we pass in the desired key using one of two syntaxes:

```
>>> cities = {"Amsterdam": 780000, "Brasilia": 2480000,
"Canberra": 360000}
>>> cities['Brasilia']
2480000
>>> cities.get('Brasilia')
2480000
```

If the key exists, these syntaxes behave identically. But if the key does *not* exist, there is a different behavior.

```
>>> cities['Dresden']
Traceback (most recent call last):
  File "<stdin>", line 1, in <module>
KeyError: 'Dresden'
>>> cities.get('Dresden')
>>> cities.get('Dresden', 0)
0
```

The get() method will return None if not found, or the default value that we specify as a second argument. The [ ] syntax will throw an exception. If you know 100% that the key exists in the dictionary, the bracket syntax is usually cleaner and more readable. However, if there's a chance that the key does not exist, you are safer using the get() method.

Add/Update

The syntax to add a key-value to a dictionary is the same syntax for updating the value of an existing key. If the key we pass exists, the value is updated. If the key does not exist, the key-value pair is added. Here's how we add Dresden:

```
>>> cities = {"Amsterdam": 780000, "Brasilia": 2480000,
"Canberra": 360000}
>>> cities
{'Amsterdam': 780000, 'Canberra': 360000, 'Brasilia': 2480000}
>>> cities['Dresden'] = 525000
>>> cities
{'Dresden': 525000, 'Amsterdam': 780000, 'Canberra': 360000,
'Brasilia': 2480000}
```

Notice that Dresden was not added to the end of the dictionary. This is because dictionaries are *unordered*. In most cases, this is fine because we simply pass a key into the dictionary and let the computer figure out how to find the value. If you need an ordered dictionary, Python does provide an OrderedDict type in the *collections module*.[2]

If we wanted to update the population of, say, Amsterdam, we use the same syntax.

```
>>> cities = {"Amsterdam": 780000, "Brasilia": 2480000,
"Canberra": 360000}
>>> cities
{'Amsterdam': 780000, 'Canberra': 360000, 'Brasilia': 2480000}
>>> cities['Amsterdam'] = 800000
>>> cities
{'Amsterdam': 800000, 'Canberra': 360000, 'Brasilia': 2480000}
```

---

[2]https://docs.python.org/3.5/library/collections.html

It may be obvious, but the implication is that you cannot store duplicate keys in a dictionary.

Delete

To remove a pair from a dictionary, use the del keyword.

```
>>> cities = {"Amsterdam": 780000, "Brasilia": 2480000,
"Canberra": 360000}
>>> cities
{'Amsterdam': 780000, 'Canberra': 360000, 'Brasilia': 2480000}
>>> del cities['Amsterdam']
>>> cities
{'Canberra': 360000, 'Brasilia': 2480000}
```

Loop

Sometimes it is useful to iterate over a dictionary in a for-each loop. Similar to the enumerate() function, we use items() to iterate over a dictionary and get back a tuple. Specifically, we get each key-value pair in the dictionary as a tuple.

```
>>> cities = {"Amsterdam": 780000, "Brasilia": 2480000,
"Canberra": 360000}
>>> for k, v in cities.items():
...     print("City: {}, Pop: {}".format(k, v))
...
City: Amsterdam, Pop: 780000
City: Canberra, Pop: 360000
City: Brasilia, Pop: 2480000
```

You may not have seen a for loop in the REPL before, but you can enter them just like any other Python code. You can even define methods and classes in the REPL. When you press Return, you will automatically see ..., which means the REPL is expecting you to complete the statement. Just remember, you need to enter indentation manually. When you're finished, press Return twice to complete the loop, function, class, etc.

Remember that the k and v in the previous example can have any name, such as city and pop, but k and v are commonly used because they stand for "key" and "value".

Limiting Actions

Currently, the player can take any action at any time, even if it doesn't make sense. For example, players could attack in the starting tile or heal when they have full health.

To start fixing this, let's add a new function to the game.py module that stores all of the legal actions in a dictionary. We'll use an OrderedDict to ensure that the actions appear in the same order to the player each time. To create an ordered dictionary, you need to add from collections import OrderedDict at the top of the module.

What we would like to do is something like this for each action:

```
1   actions = OrderedDict()
2   if player.inventory:
3       actions['i'] = player.print_inventory
4       actions['I'] = player.print_inventory
5       print("i: View inventory")
```

First we check a condition. In this case, we check if the player has an inventory (remember, if `my_list` is the same as if `my_list != []`). Second, we map the upper- and lowercase hotkeys to that action. Last, we print the action to the user. There's a very important syntax difference here that is easy to miss: We do *not* write `player.print_inventory()`, we write `player.print_inventory`. As we've seen before, `my_function()` is the syntax to execute a function. If instead we just want to *refer* to the function, we use the function name without `()`. This is important because we don't want to *do* the actions right now, we just want to store the possible actions in the dictionary.[3]

Since we're going to need to do this for a bunch of actions, we'll also create a helper function, called `action_adder()`.

```
29   def get_available_actions(room, player):
30       actions = OrderedDict()
31       print("Choose an action: ")
32       if player.inventory:
33           action_adder(actions, 'i', player.print_inventory,
                 "Print inventory")
34       if isinstance(room, world.EnemyTile) and room.enemy.
             is_alive():
35           action_adder(actions, 'a', player.attack,
                 "Attack")
36       else:
37           if world.tile_at(room.x, room.y - 1):
38               action_adder(actions, 'n', player.move_north,
                     "Go north")
39           if world.tile_at(room.x, room.y + 1):
```

---

[3]This feature of Python is very handy, but a lot of languages do not support it. In Python, functions are "first-class objects," which means that they can be passed around and modified just like strings, integers, or `MapTiles`.

```
40              action_adder(actions, 's', player.move_south,
                    "Go south")
41          if world.tile_at(room.x + 1, room.y):
42              action_adder(actions, 'e', player.move_east,
                    "Go east")
43          if world.tile_at(room.x - 1, room.y):
44              action_adder(actions, 'w', player.move_west,
                    "Go west")
45      if player.hp < 100:
46          action_adder(actions, 'h', player.heal, "Heal")
47
48      return actions
49
50  def action_adder(action_dict, hotkey, action, name):
51      action_dict[hotkey.lower()] = action
52      action_dict[hotkey.upper()] = action
53      print("{}: {}".format(hotkey, name))
```

Now at any time, we can call get_available_actions() to create a
dictionary of hotkey-action pairs. To utilize the dictionary, create another
new function.

```
17  def choose_action(room, player):
18      action = None
19      while not action:
20          available_actions = get_available_actions(room,
                player)
21          action_input = input("Action: ")
22          action = available_actions.get(action_input)
23          if action:
24              action()
25          else:
26              print("Invalid action!")
```

We've seen this pattern before: we keep looping until we get valid input from the user. However, these three lines need some explanation:

```
22    action = available_actions.get(action_input)
23    if action:
24        action()
```

We use get() instead of the [] syntax because it's possible the user entered an invalid hotkey. The if action line is shorthand for if action != None or if action is not None. If a function was found, we execute that function by adding the parentheses: action(). The important distinction here is that action is just a reference to the function, whereas action() runs the function.

Having added this new function, we can delete get_player_command() and we can clean up play() as follows:

```
6     def play():
7         print("Escape from Cave Terror!")
8         player = Player()
9         while True:
10            room = world.tile_at(player.x, player.y)
11            print(room.intro_text())
12            room.modify_player(player)
13            choose_action(room, player)
```

If you play the game now, you will see that the player's actions are limited based on context. Okay, so we can scratch a few bugs off the list! We should take this opportunity to do some refactoring.

Expanding the World

At present, our world is pretty small. Small enough that our world_map is still fairly readable and maintainable. But if it gets much larger, making changes is going to be very frustrating. We also have the annoyance of specifying the X-Y coordinates for each tile manually.

Sometimes, when programs require a particular section of the code to be flexible and more maintainable than the language provides, programmers use *domain specific languages* (DSL). A DSL is written in a way that is particular to the problem at hand; hence it is a *language* that is *specific* to the *domain*.

We'll use a DSL to define the map for our world and then Python code to interpret the DSL and turn it into the world_map variable. Since the map is a grid, it would be nice if the DSL reflected that. Usually, a DSL has some features of full programming languages, but our domain is so simple that a string will serve our purposes. Let's start sketching out some ideas of what the DSL could look like and then we'll write the code to interpret it.

A first go might look something like this:

```
1   world_dsl = """
2   ||VictoryTile||
3   ||EnemyTile||
4   |EnemyTile|StartTile|EnemyTile|
5   ||EnemyTile||
6   """
```

Each new line of the string is a row in the map, and each tile within the row is separated by a | (pipe) character. If there is no tile, we just put two pipes next to each other. I like the idea here and it does remove the X-Y coordinates, but it still visually looks a bit wonky. What if we tried making it look more grid-like?

```
1    world_dsl = """
2    |            |VictoryTile|            |
3    |            |EnemyTile|              |
4    |EnemyTile|StartTile|EnemyTile|
5    |            |EnemyTile|              |
6    """
```

Hmm, that's better, but it still doesn't quite line up. Also, it's pretty wide, which means a large map could still be hard to read. What if we shortened those names?

```
1    world_dsl = """
2    | |VT| |
3    | |EN| |
4    |EN|ST|EN|
5    | |EN| |
6    """
```

To me, this is an improvement because you can clearly see the layout of the map, and it looks like a grid. The trade-off is we have to use abbreviations for the tile types. I think this should be okay because even after we add more tile types, we will only have about 5-10 types to keep track of. If we had dozens of tile types, the abbreviations might get too difficult to keep track of, and we might choose a different format. For now, go ahead and add this world_dsl variable to the world.py module right above the world_map variable.

When we run Python code, the Python interpreter has all sorts of checks in place to prevent us from doing something wrong. Among other things, it validates syntax and prevents the program from running if there is a syntax error. Since DSLs are invented for a specific program, they don't come with any error checking in place. Can you imagine trying to chase down a bug in a Python program only to find out it was a syntax error? For our own sanity, we should add some simple error checking for the DSL.

Let's start by checking these three basics:

- There should be exactly one start tile

- There should be at least one victory tile

- Each row should have the same number of cells

To help us do this, we will use two string methods: count() and splitlines(). The count() method works just as you would expect: it counts the number of occurrences of some substring in a string. The splitlines() method breaks apart a multiline string wherever there is a new line and returns a list of the lines. Bearing that in mind, here is the validation function.

```
81   def is_dsl_valid(dsl):
82       if dsl.count("|ST|") != 1:
83           return False
84       if dsl.count("|VT|") == 0:
85           return False
86       lines = dsl.splitlines()
87       lines = [l for l in lines if l]
88       pipe_counts = [line.count("|") for line in lines]
89       for count in pipe_counts:
90           if count != pipe_counts[0]:
91               return False
92
93       return True
```

Since dsl is a string, we can right away count the number of start tiles and victory tiles to make sure those requirements are met. To check the number of tiles in each row, we first need to split the string into rows. Once split into rows, we use a list comprehension to filter out any empty lines (there should be one empty line at the beginning and end because we used

the triple-quote string syntax). Remember that if l is shorthand for if
l != ''. Once filtered, we use a second list comprehension to count the
number of pipes in each row, and then make sure that every row has the
same number of pipes as the first row. If any of those conditions fail, the
function immediately returns False.

Next, we need to add the function that builds up the world_map
variable using the DSL. For starters, we need to define a dictionary that
maps DSL abbreviations to tile types.

```
95    tile_type_dict = {"VT": VictoryTile,
96                       "EN": EnemyTile,
97                       "ST": StartTile,
98                       "  ": None}
```

Take note that we are mapping the abbreviations to tile *types* not tile
objects. The difference between EnemyTile and EnemyTile(1,5) is that the
former is a type and the latter is a new instance of the type. This is similar
to how go_north is a reference to a function and go_north() calls the
function.

Since we are now going to programmatically build up world_map,
replace the existing map with world_map = []. Below that, we will add the
function to parse the DSL. In general, the function will validate the DSL, go
line by line and cell by cell looking up the mappings for the abbreviations,
and create new tile objects based on the tile type it finds.

```
104    def parse_world_dsl():
105        if not is_dsl_valid(world_dsl):
106            raise SyntaxError("DSL is invalid!")
107
108        dsl_lines = world_dsl.splitlines()
109        dsl_lines = [x for x in dsl_lines if x]
110
111        for y, dsl_row in enumerate(dsl_lines):
```

```
112            row = []
113            dsl_cells = dsl_row.split("|")
114            dsl_cells = [c for c in dsl_cells if c]
115            for x, dsl_cell in enumerate(dsl_cells):
116                tile_type = tile_type_dict[dsl_cell]
117                row.append(tile_type(x, y) if tile_type else
                   None)
118
119            world_map.append(row)
```

You should also call this new function in game.py.

```
6   def play():
7       print("Escape from Cave Terror!")
8       world.parse_world_dsl()
9       player = Player()
10      while True:
11          room = world.tile_at(player.x, player.y)
12          print(room.intro_text())
13          room.modify_player(player)
14          choose_action(room, player)
```

Let's review in detail what the function does. First, the DSL is validated and if it is invalid, we raise a SyntaxError. This is another example of an exception that we will intentionally raise to alert the programmer that they did something wrong. Next, just like before, we split the DSL into lines and remove the empty lines created by the triple-quote syntax. The last part of the function actually creates the world. It is a little dense, so I will explain each line:

```
1   # Iterate over each line in the DSL.
2   # Instead of i, the variable y is used because
3   # we're working with an X-Y grid.
```

```
4   for y, dsl_row in enumerate(dsl_lines):
5       # Create an object to store the tiles
6       row = []
7       # Split the line into abbreviations using
8       # the "split" method
9       dsl_cells = dsl_row.split("|")
10      # The split method includes the beginning
11      # and end of the line so we need to remove
12      # those nonexistent cells
13      dsl_cells = [c for c in dsl_cells if c]
14      # Iterate over each cell in the DSL line
15      # Instead of j, the variable x is used because
16      # we're working with an X-Y grid.
17      for x, dsl_cell in enumerate(dsl_cells):
18          # Look up the abbreviation in the dictionary
19          tile_type = tile_type_dict[dsl_cell]
20          # If the dictionary returned a valid type, create
21          # a new tile object, pass it the X-Y coordinates
22          # as required by the tile __init__(), and add
23          # it to the row object. If None was found in the
24          # dictionary, we just add None.
25          row.append(tile_type(x, y) if tile_type else None)
26      # Add the whole row to the world_map
27      world_map.append(row)
```

The syntax `value_if_true` *if* condition *else* `value_if_false` is a slightly different way of writing an `if` statement when you simply need to toggle a value based on a boolean expression. As in the example `row.append(tile_type(x, y) if tile_type else None)`, it can condense what would otherwise be a multi-line code block into one line. This syntax is sometimes referred to as a *ternary*.

While this took a lot of work, the game is relatively unchanged from the player's perspective. Such is the lot of the refactoring developer! But don't worry, this wasn't for naught. This work was done to make our lives easier. Now, expanding the map is trivial and even a 20x20 world would be easy to view and edit.

There were a lot of changes to the nuts and bolts of the application, so you might have a few errors here and there. Be sure to review your code closely and compare it to the code bundled with the book if you get stuck.

CHAPTER 14

Econ 101

Much like we turned the crusty bread into something more than a string, this chapter will focus on making gold a real commodity in the game. After all, what adventure would be complete without the ability to buy and sell loot?

Share the Wealth

While it would be possible to track gold as an actual item, that could get out of hand if the player has lots of it. Instead, it's easier to handle gold separately from items and simply have a statistic associated with the players that can grow or shrink. Update the __init__() function of the Player class to move gold out of the inventory list.

```
4    class Player:
5        def __init__(self):
6            self.inventory = [items.Rock(),
7                                items.Dagger(),
8                                items.CrustyBread()]
9            self.x = world.start_tile_location[0]
10           self.y = world.start_tile_location[1]
11           self.hp = 100
12           self.gold = 5
```

© Phillip Johnson 2018
P. Johnson, *Make Your Own Python Text Adventure*,
https://doi.org/10.1007/978-1-4842-3231-6_14

We should also update the `print_inventory()` method to let the players know how much gold they have.

```
14    def print_inventory(self):
15        print("Inventory:")
16        for item in self.inventory:
17            print('* ' + str(item))
18        print("Gold: {}".format(self.gold))
```

Now that the players have money to spend, we should make it meaningful by adding a `value` attribute to the items in the game. Here's the `RustySword` class with a `value`.

```
26    class RustySword(Weapon):
27        def __init__(self):
28            self.name = "Rusty sword"
29            self.description = "This sword is showing its age, " \
30                                "but still has some fight in
it."
31            self.damage = 20
32            self.value = 100
```

You will also need to add a value for the other items. Here are the values I chose.

Class	Value
Rock	1
Dagger	20
RustySword	100
CrustyBread	12

Customization Point   Change the values of the items to make them more or less desirable.

While we're at it, let's add another item: a HealingPotion that is a bit stronger and more valuable than crusty bread.

```
49    class HealingPotion(Consumable):
50        def __init__(self):
51            self.name = "Healing Potion"
52            self.healing_value = 50
53            self.value = 60
```

Of course, the players need someone to trade with in order for the game to have an economy. To introduce other characters into the game, we're going to create a new npc.py module. We'll use the all-familiar pattern—the generic base class and specific subclass—to define the Trader class.

npc.py

```
1    import items
2
3
4    class NonPlayableCharacter():
5        def __init__(self):
6            raise NotImplementedError("Do not create raw NPC
             objects.")
7
8        def __str__(self):
9            return self.name
10
11
```

```
12   class Trader(NonPlayableCharacter):
13       def __init__(self):
14           self.name = "Trader"
15           self.gold = 100
16           self.inventory = [items.CrustyBread(),
17                             items.CrustyBread(),
18                             items.CrustyBread(),
19                             items.HealingPotion(),
20                             items.HealingPotion()]
```

✎ Customization Point   Change the items the Trader has in its inventory. A more difficult game could have fewer Consumables and an easier game might have a wide selection of Consumables and Weapons.

Giving the Trader a Home

Just like the EnemyTiles that have an Enemy object, we're going to create a TraderTile that has a Trader object. (Don't forget to import npc!)

```
98    class TraderTile(MapTile):
99        def __init__(self, x, y):
100           self.trader = npc.Trader()
101           super().__init__(x, y)
```

To handle the business of buying and selling, we'll add a trade() method to this class. This method will show all of the items available to trade (i.e., the seller's inventory), ask the player to choose an item, and finally complete the trade if the player makes a choice.

When I first drafted the class, I used a buy() and sell() method. However, it became apparent that these two methods were extremely similar. To avoid duplicating code, I revised my original plan of using two methods and instead used a general "trade" method where one person is the buyer and one person is the seller. If the player is buying, the trader is selling, and if the player is selling, the trader is buying. This process is known as *abstraction* and abstracting code to more general patterns is usually a good idea because it makes the code more reusable. Learning to abstract takes practice and sometimes, as in this example, it takes writing out some code before the abstraction reveals itself.

```
118    def trade(self, buyer, seller):
119        for i, item in enumerate(seller.inventory, 1):
120            print("{}. {} - {} Gold".format(i, item.name,
               item.value))
121        while True:
122            user_input = input("Choose an item or press Q to
               exit: ")
123            if user_input in ['Q', 'q']:
124                return
125            else:
126                try:
127                    choice = int(user_input)
128                    to_swap = seller.inventory[choice - 1]
129                    self.swap(seller, buyer, to_swap)
130                except ValueError:
131                    print("Invalid choice!")
```

This method uses what looks like an infinite loop (while True), but you will notice that if the player chooses to quit without making a trade, the return keyword is used to exit the method. This method also makes a call to the swap() method, which has not yet been written, but we'll add that now.

```
133    def swap(self, seller, buyer, item):
134        if item.value > buyer.gold:
135            print("That's too expensive")
136            return
137        seller.inventory.remove(item)
138        buyer.inventory.append(item)
139        seller.gold = seller.gold + item.value
140        buyer.gold = buyer.gold - item.value
141        print("Trade complete!")
```

This method simply removes the item from the seller, gives it to the buyer, and then does the reverse with the gold value of the item traded. Since this function works "both ways," we need a way for the players to initiate if they want to buy or sell items. The method check_if_trade() will accept user input to control who the buyers and sellers are.

```
103    def check_if_trade(self, player):
104        while True:
105            print("Would you like to (B)uy, (S)ell, or (Q)uit?")
106            user_input = input()
107            if user_input in ['Q', 'q']:
108                return
109            elif user_input in ['B', 'b']:
110                print("Here's whats available to buy: ")
111                self.trade(buyer=player, seller=self.trader)
112            elif user_input in ['S', 's']:
```

```
113              print("Here's whats available to sell: ")
114              self.trade(buyer=self.trader, seller=player)
115          else:
116              print("Invalid choice!")
```

This method also uses a seemingly infinite loop, but exits using return when the player is done trading. Depending on the player's choice, the player object is passed to trade() as either the buyer or seller. Named parameters are used to make it explicitly clear who is who.

Finally, we need to give this room its intro text:

```
144   def intro_text(self):
145       return """
146       A frail not-quite-human, not-quite-creature squats in
          the corner
147       clinking his gold coins together. He looks willing to
          trade.
148       """
```

To let the player initiate trading, we need to create an action in the Player class and then add it to the list of available actions. Add this method to the bottom of the Player class in player.py.

```
83   def trade(self):
84       room = world.tile_at(self.x, self.y)
85       room.check_if_trade(self)
```

Now, switch to game.py and add this check to see if the player is in a TraderTile.

```
32   if player.inventory:
33       action_adder(actions, 'i', player.print_inventory,
         "Print inventory")
34   if isinstance(room, world.TraderTile):
```

```
35        action_adder(actions, 't', player.trade, "Trade")
36    if isinstance(room, world.EnemyTile) and room.enemy.is_
      alive():
37        action_adder(actions, 'a', player.attack, "Attack")
```

Expanding the World

To make the store concept usable to the players, we also need to give players the opportunity to increase their wealth. We'll create one more tile type in world.py: FindGoldTile. This tile will have a random amount of gold to find and a boolean that tracks if the gold has been picked up. This boolean variable ensures that players can't just enter and exit the room repeatedly to infinitely increase their wealth!

```
75    class FindGoldTile(MapTile):
76        def __init__(self, x, y):
77            self.gold = random.randint(1, 50)
78            self.gold_claimed = False
79            super().__init__(x, y)
80
81        def modify_player(self, player):
82            if not self.gold_claimed:
83                self.gold_claimed = True
84                player.gold = player.gold + self.gold
85                print("+{} gold added.".format(self.gold))
86
87        def intro_text(self):
88            if self.gold_claimed:
89                return """
90                Another unremarkable part of the cave. You
                  must forge onwards.
```

```
91              """
92          else:
93              return """
94              Someone dropped some gold. You pick it up.
95              """
```

The new function here is random.randint(). Unlike random.random(), which returns a decimal number, random.randint() returns an integer in the given range.

With two new tile types, we can grow the game world and add some more interest to the game. Here's the layout I chose:

```
150    world_dsl = """
151    |EN|EN|VT|EN|EN|
152    |EN|  |  |  |EN|
153    |EN|FG|EN|  |TT|
154    |TT|  |ST|FG|EN|
155    |FG|  |EN|  |FG|
156    """
```

✐ Customization Point   Change the layout of the game world in any way you like. Just make sure it meets the DSL requirements or you'll get a SyntaxError.

In order to make sure our DSL still works, we need to add the new tile abbreviations to the dictionary.

```
173    tile_type_dict = {"VT": VictoryTile,
174                      "EN": EnemyTile,
175                      "ST": StartTile,
```

```
176                         "FG": FindGoldTile,
177                         "TT": TraderTile,
178                         "  ": None}
```

If you ran the game now, you would run into some issues because the starting tile moved. Ideally, we'd like to be able to tweak the DSL without manually adjusting the start location in the Player class. Since there is only one StartTile (we enforced that in is_dsl_valid()), it would be easy to record its location during parsing and then use that value in the Player class. In order to record the location, we'll need a new variable in the world.py module called start_tile_location. That variable will be set in the parse_world_dsl() function.

```
183     start_tile_location = None
184
185     def parse_world_dsl():
186         if not is_dsl_valid(world_dsl):
187             raise SyntaxError("DSL is invalid!")
188
189         dsl_lines = world_dsl.splitlines()
190         dsl_lines = [x for x in dsl_lines if x]
191
192         for y, dsl_row in enumerate(dsl_lines):
193             row = []
194             dsl_cells = dsl_row.split("|")
195             dsl_cells = [c for c in dsl_cells if c]
196             for x, dsl_cell in enumerate(dsl_cells):
197                 tile_type = tile_type_dict[dsl_cell]
198                 if tile_type == StartTile:
199                     global start_tile_location
200                     start_tile_location = x, y
```

```
201            row.append(tile_type(x, y) if tile_type else
               None)
202
203        world_map.append(row)
```

You should have noticed that before the variable is set, we have to include a `global start_tile_location` line. The `global` keyword allows us to access a variable at the module level from inside a function. Variables declared at the module level are considered "global" because any part of the application that uses the module has access to the variable. In general, modifying global variables can have unwanted consequences, especially if other modules are relying on that variable. So the `global` keyword is a way of forcing the programmer to be clear about their intent to modify a global variable. If we wanted to avoid using a global variable, we could make `start_tile_location` a function that parses the DSL and returns the start location. However, I think that would introduce unnecessary complexity in the code. The use of this global variable is very limited and we know it will just be set once and accessed once. Global variables are not evil; they just need treated with some extra care.

When we set the `start_tile_location` variable, we use the tuple syntax to store both x and y in the variable. Knowing that the coordinates are stored in that way, we can reference them from the `Player` class in `player.py`.

```
4    class Player:
5        def __init__(self):
6            self.inventory = [items.Rock(),
7                               items.Dagger(),
8                               items.CrustyBread()]
9            self.x = world.start_tile_location[0]
10           self.y = world.start_tile_location[1]
11           self.hp = 100
12           self.gold = 5
```

Tuple values can be accessed via indexes just like lists. Since we know the variable is stored as (x, y), the value at index 0 is the X-coordinate and the value at index 1 is the Y-coordinate.[1] This code relies on the world having been created first, otherwise start_tile_location would still be None. Thankfully in game.py, we parse the DSL before creating the player object.

This last change made the DSL fully decoupled from the rest of the game because the game doesn't have to "know" anything specific about the DSL. Usually, the more decoupled parts of an application are, the better. Decoupling allows you to change one part of an application without changing another part. In this application, it means you can revise the world map at any time without having to change another part of the code.

✎ Customization Point   Add some new tile types. Maybe you could have a FindItemTile, an InstantDeathTile, or a BossTile with a particularly difficult enemy.

---

[1]If you feel like accessing tuple values via index is a little kludgy, you wouldn't be wrong. Python has an alternative called *named tuples* (see https://docs. python.org/3.5/library/collections.html#collections.namedtuple) that could also work in the situation if you prefer.

CHAPTER 15

Endgame

We made it! Much like you can claim victory over learning some Python, our game players will soon be able to claim victory too. We need to add just one more feature so that the game ends when the player dies or reaches the victory tile.

Finishing Up

We can start by modifying the Player class in player.py to add a victory property and an is_alive() method.

```
5    class Player:
6        def __init__(self):
7            self.inventory = [items.Rock(),
8                                  items.Dagger(),
9                                  items.CrustyBread()]
10           self.x = world.start_tile_location[0]
11           self.y = world.start_tile_location[1]
12           self.hp = 100
13           self.gold = 5
14           self.victory = False
15
16       def is_alive(self):
17           return self.hp > 0
```

© Phillip Johnson 2018
P. Johnson, *Make Your Own Python Text Adventure,*
https://doi.org/10.1007/978-1-4842-3231-6_15

We should set the victory property to true in the VictoryTile in world.py.

```
64    class VictoryTile(MapTile):
65        def modify_player(self, player):
66            player.victory = True
67
68        def intro_text(self):
69            return """
70            You see a bright light in the distance...
71            ... it grows as you get closer! It's sunlight!
72
73
74            Victory is yours!
75            """
```

Next we need to adjust the condition of our game loop in game.py so that it checks to see if the player is alive or if victory has been achieved. In the play method, change while True to while player.is_alive() and not player.victory. Another way to phrase this condition would be "keep going until the player dies or wins."

We also need to add an check after modify_player() runs since that function could cause the player to win or lose. Finally, we should let the player know if they die. Here's the complete play() method.

```
6     def play():
7         print("Escape from Cave Terror!")
8         world.parse_world_dsl()
9         player = Player()
10        while player.is_alive() and not player.victory:
11            room = world.tile_at(player.x, player.y)
12            print(room.intro_text())
13            room.modify_player(player)
```

```
14          if player.is_alive() and not player.victory:
15              choose_action(room, player)
16          elif not player.is_alive():
17              print("Your journey has come to an early end!")
```

You can now play through the game and it will end if you die or when you reach a victory tile.

What Next?

First, take a moment to congratulate yourself. You went from knowing nothing about Python to having a complete working game. But my guess is you want to do more than just build the game I put together. This section contains some suggestions of what to do next.

Add More Features to the Game

Your imagination is the limit of what you could do in the text adventure. Here are some ideas:

- Add another NPC who can give a quest. Then, add another tile type where the player completes the quest.

- Make enemies have loot that can be retrieved after killing them.

- Give the player magic attacks that deplete mana. Allow mana to replenish a little bit each time the player moves into a room and/or with a potion.

- Allow the player to wear armor that reduces enemy attacks by a percentage.

Make Your Job Easier with Python Scripts

Python is a great language to write small scripts that automate boring tasks. Modifying spreadsheets, fetching data from web sites, etc. For more guidance, take a look at Automate the Boring Stuff with Python[1] by Al Sweigart.

Write a Web Application

It's easier than you think, especially with Python. Since I assume you are new to programming, I recommend the Udacity course *How to Build a Blog*[2] by Steve Huffman (of Reddit fame). This course teaches web development fundamentals using Python.

There's much, much more to learn about Python and I encourage you to keep learning. There are many beginner-friendly resources available, no matter where your interests lie. Happy coding!

---

[1]https://automatetheboringstuff.com
[2]https://www.udacity.com/course/web-development--cs253

APPENDIX A

Homework Solutions

The solutions in this appendix should only be consulted after giving the homework questions a fair shot. If you're stuck, compare your code against the solution code and make sure you can follow the logic in the solution.

You may also be comparing your code against the solutions to see if you solved the problem in the right way. While I encourage this, each solution represents just one possible way of solving the problem. In general, code should be correct, readable, and efficient—in that order. Your code may be different, but still meet those goals. If your code *is* different, try to see if you can learn something from my solutions. You may even find that your solution is better than mine. There are always multiple ways to solve a problem and as long as we keep learning from each other, we're doing the right thing.

Chapter 2: Your First Program

1. Make a new module called `calculator.py` and write code that will print out `"Which numbers do you want to add?"` to the console.

    calculator.py

    ```
    1   print("Which numbers do you want to add?")
    ```

© Phillip Johnson 2018
P. Johnson, *Make Your Own Python Text Adventure*,
https://doi.org/10.1007/978-1-4842-3231-6_16

2. Run the calculator program and make sure it works correctly.

```
1    $ python calculator.py
2    Which numbers do you want to add?
```

3. Try removing the quotes from the code. What happens?

```
1    $ python calculator.py
2      File "calculator.py", line 1
3        print(What numbers do you want to add?)
4                      ^
5    SyntaxError: invalid syntax
```

Chapter 3: Listening to Your Users

1. What *is* the difference between `my_variable = 5` and `my_variable = '5'`?

    The first is the actual number five, whereas the second is just the text character "5".

2. What is the difference between `print(n)` and `print('n')`?

    The first will try to print out the value of the variable n, whereas the second will just print out the character "n".

3. Try rewriting `echo.py` without using a variable.

    echo.py

```
1    print(input("Type some text: "))
```

Chapter 4: Decisions

1. What is the difference between = and ==?

    The = operator assigns values to variables, whereas
    the == operator compares two values to see if they
    are equal.

2. Create ages.py to ask users their age and then print
    out information related to their age. For example,
    if that person is an adult, if they can buy alcohol,
    if they can vote, etc. Note: The int() function can
    convert a string to an integer.

    This is one example; yours will be different:

    ages.py

```
1   age = int(input("What is your age? "))
2   if age < 18:
3       print("You are a child.")
4   elif 18 < age < 21:
5       print("You are an adult, but you cannot
        purchase alcohol.")
6   else:
7       print("You are an adult.")
8   if age >= 16:
9       print("You are allowed to drive.")
10  else:
11      print("You are not allowed to drive")
```

Chapter 5: Functions

1. What keyword is used to create a function?

   The def keyword.

2. What are some differences between parameterless and parameterized functions?

   The functions are called differently in code.
   A call to do_domething() is parameterless and a call to do_something(a, b) is parameterized.
   A parameterized function requires input to do its work, whereas a parameterless function already has access to everything it needs to do its work.

3. When reading the code for a function, how do you know if it just "does something" or "gives something back"?

   If the function contains the return keyword followed by a value, then it gives something back.

4. Create doubler.py to contain one function named double that accepts a single parameter. The function should return the input value multiplied by two. Print out the doubled value of 12345 and 1.57.

   doubler.py

   ```
   1    def double(a):
   2        return a * 2
   3
   4    print(double(12345))
   5    print(double(1.57))
   ```

5. Create `calculator.py` to contain one function named add that accepts two parameters. The function should return the sum of the two numbers. Print out the sum of 45 and 55.

calculator.py

```
1   def add(a, b):
2       return a + b
3
4   print(add(45, 55))
```

6. Create `user_calculator.py` and re-use your add function from the previous exercise. This time, ask the user for two numbers and print the sum of those numbers. Hint: It is okay if this works only with integers.

user_calculator.py

```
1   def add(a, b):
2       return a + b
3
4   num1 = int(input("Please enter your 1st number: "))
5   num2 = int(input("Please enter your 2nd number: "))
6
7   print(add(num1, num2))
```

Chapter 6: Lists

1. What two characteristics make a collection a list?

    Lists are ordered and they may contain duplicates.

2. Write a script called favorites.py that allows users to enter their three favorite foods. Store those foods in a list.

favorites.py

```
1   favorites = []
2   favorites.append(input("What is your favorite
    food? "))
3   favorites.append(input("What is your 2nd favorite
    food? "))
4   favorites.append(input("What is your 3rd favorite
    food? "))
```

3. Print out the middle item of this list using an index: ['Mercury', 'Venus', 'Earth']. Could you change your code to work with a list of any size (assuming there are an odd number of items)? Hint: Think back to the int function that converts something into an integer.

```
1   planets = ['Mercury', 'Venus', 'Earth']
2   print(planets[1])
```

Or

```
1   planets = ['Mercury', 'Venus', 'Earth']
2   middle_index = int(len(planets) / 2)
3   print(planets[middle_index])
```

4. What happens when you run this code? Do you know why?

An `IndexError: list index out of range` is thrown. This happens because list indices are zero-based. The first item is at index 0 and the last is at index 2, but we asked for index 3 because the list contains three items.

Chapter 7: Loops

1. What kind of loop would you use for each of the following:

    A. A program that checks the temperature every five seconds

        A `while` loop because the program needs to keep running with no defined end.

    B. A program that prints receipts at grocery stores

        A for-each loop because we want to print each of the items the customer purchased. (Technically, a while loop can also be used, but a for-each loop is more idiomatic.)

    C. A program that tallies the score in a bowling game

        A `for-each` loop because we want to go through each of the ten rounds in the game to find the final score. (Technically, a `while` loop can also be used, but a `for-each` loop is more idiomatic.)

D. A program that randomly shuffles and plays songs from a music library

A while loop because we don't know how long the user is going to run the program. You might be tempted to use a for-each loop to go through each of the songs in the library, but what if the users want to keep playing music even after they have gone through all their songs?

2. Open user_calculator.py from Chapter 5 on functions and add a while loop that allows the user to keep adding two numbers.

user_calculator.py

```
1    def add(a, b):
2        return a + b
3
4    while True:
5        num1 = int(input("Please enter your
         1st number: "))
6        num2 = int(input("Please enter your
         2nd number: "))
7
8        print(add(num1, num2))
```

3. Write a script that displays a multiplication table from 1 * 1 to 10 * 10.

multiplication.py

```
1    for i in range(1, 11):
2        line = ""
3        for j in range(1, 11):
```

```
4              line = line + str(i * j) + " "
5        print(line)
```

4. Use enumerate and the % operator to print every third word in this list.

greek.py

```
1    letters = ['alpha','beta','gamma','delta',
     'epsilon','zeta','eta']
2    for i, letter in enumerate(letters):
3        if i % 3 == 0:
4            print(letter)
```

Chapter 8: Objects

1. What is the difference between a class and an object?

   A class is the template in code that defines the data elements for the "thing" the class represents. An object is a specific instance of a class that lives in memory when the program runs.

2. What is the purpose of an __init__() method in a class?

   It runs as soon as the object is created and is commonly used to set the values of members in the class.

3. What is the difference between __str__() and
    str()?

    __str()__ is a method that can be defined in a
    class that tells Python how to print the objects made
    from that class and how to represent those objects
    as strings. str() is a built-in function that tries to
    convert an object into a string.

4. Create a file called food.py that contains a class
    called Food. This class should have four members:
    name, carbs, protein, and fat. These members
    should be set in the initializer of the class.

    food.py

```
1   class Food:
2       def __init__(self, name, carbs, protein, fat):
3           self.name = name
4           self.carbs = carbs
5           self.protein = protein
6           self.fat = fat
```

5. Add a method to the Food class called calories()
    that calculates the number of calories in the food.
    There are 4 calories per gram of carbs, 4 calories per
    gram of protein, and 9 calories per gram of fat.

    food.py

```
1   def calories(self):
2       return self.carbs * 4 + self.protein
        * 4 + self.fat * 9
```

6. Create another class called Recipe that has an initializer that accepts a name and a list of food items called ingredients. Add a method to this class called calories() that returns the total calories in the recipe.

food.py

```
1    class Recipe:
2        def __init__(self, name, ingredients):
3            self.name = name
4            self.ingredients = ingredients
5
6    def calories(self):
7        total = 0
8        for ingredient in self.ingredients:
9            total = total + ingredient.calories()
10
11        return total
```

7. Add a __str__() method to the Recipe class that simply returns the name of the recipe.

food.py

```
1    def __str__(self):
2        return self.name
```

8. Create two (simple!) recipes and print out the name
    and total calories for each recipe. You can make
    up the numbers for carbs, protein, and fat if you
    choose. For bonus points, try to do this in a way that
    would work for two recipes or 200 recipes.

    In the following answer, I used a feature called
    named arguments to clarify which number is fat,
    protein, etc. This is not required, but I wanted to
    show you an option to make arguments clearer when
    you have a lot of them. My solution "works for two
    recipes or 200" because it stores each recipe in a list
    and then uses a loop to print everything in the list.

food.py

```
1   pbj = Recipe("Peanut Butter & Jelly", [
2       Food(name="Peanut Butter", carbs=6, protein=8,
        fat=16),
3       Food(name="Jelly", carbs=13, protein=0,
        fat=0),
4       Food(name="Bread", carbs=24, protein=7,
        fat=2)]
5   )
6
7   omelette = Recipe("Omelette du Fromage", [
8       Food(name="Eggs", carbs=3, protein=18,
        fat=15),
9       Food(name="Cheese", carbs=5, protein=24,
        fat=24)
10  ])
11
```

```
12   recipes = [pbj, omelette]
13
14   for recipe in recipes:
15       print("{}: {} calories".format(recipe.name,
             recipe.calories()))
```

9. Are the classes in this script an example of
   inheritance or composition and why?

   Composition. A Recipe doesn't share any behavior
   with the Food objects, but a Recipe does *contain*
   Food objects.

Chapter 9: Exceptions

1. Update user_calculator.py with try and except to
   handle a user who doesn't enter a number.

   user_calculator.py

```
1    def add(a, b):
2        return a + b
3
4    while True:
5        try:
6            num1 = int(input("Please enter your 1st
                 number: "))
7            num2 = int(input("Please enter your 2nd
                 number: "))
8
9            print(add(num1, num2))
10       except ValueError:
11           print("You must enter a number.")
```

2. What does None mean and when is it used?

    The keyword None represents the absence of a value
    and it is used when we want to create a variable with
    no value.

3. What does pass mean and when is it used?

    The keyword pass means "ignore this code block". It
    can be used in any code block that does not have a
    body, such as an empty class or method or also in an
    ignored exception.

4. Create a Vehicle class, a Motorcycle class that is a
    subclass of Vehicle with a wheels attribute set to
    2, and a Car class that is a subclass of Vehicle with
    a wheels attribute set to 4. Add code that will raise
    an exception if the programmer tries to create a
    Vehicle.

    vehicles.py

```
1    class Vehicle:
2        def __init__(self):
3            raise NotImplementedError("You must use a
             subclass.")
4
5
6    class Motorcycle(Vehicle):
7        def __init__(self):
8            self.wheels = 2
9
10
11   class Car(Vehicle):
12       def __init__(self):
13           self.wheels = 4
```

APPENDIX B

Common Errors

We all want to be perfect programmers, but of course that's not possible! Here's a list of errors others have run into and how you can fix them.

AttributeError

```
AttributeError: 'NoneType' object has no attribute 'intro_text'
```

Check your *world map* and *player location*. This error means the player has moved into a None spot in the map. That shouldn't happen, so either your player is somewhere you don't expect, or your map isn't properly configured.

NameError

```
NameError: name 'enemies' is not defined (or player, world, etc.)
```

Check your *imports*. This error means Python sees the name of something that it doesn't understand. In order for Python to understand enemies (or any other module), it has to be included in an import statement at the top of the file.

© Phillip Johnson 2018
P. Johnson, *Make Your Own Python Text Adventure,*
https://doi.org/10.1007/978-1-4842-3231-6_17

TypeError

`TypeError: super() takes at least 1 argument (0 given)`

Use *Python 3.X.* You can get this error if you are using Python 2. If you're not sure which version you are using, review "Setting Up Your Workspace" in Chapter 1.

Index

© Phillip Johnson 2018
P. Johnson, *Make Your Own Python Text Adventure*,
https://doi.org/10.1007/978-1-4842-3231-6

Get the eBook for only $5!

Why limit yourself?

With most of our titles available in both PDF and ePUB format, you can access your content wherever and however you wish—on your PC, phone, tablet, or reader.

Since you've purchased this print book, we are happy to offer you the eBook for just $5.

To learn more, go to http://www.apress.com/companion or contact support@apress.com.

Apress®